DIVERSITY AT KAIZEN MOTORS

*Gender, Race, Age, and Insecurity
in a Japanese Auto Transplant*

**Darina Lepadatu
and
Thomas Janoski**

University Press of America,® Inc.
Lanham · Boulder · New York · Toronto · Plymouth, UK

**Copyright © 2011 by
University Press of America,® Inc.**
4501 Forbes Boulevard
Suite 200
Lanham, Maryland 20706
UPA Acquisitions Department (301) 459-3366

Estover Road
Plymouth PL6 7PY
United Kingdom

Library of Congress Control Number: 2011929055
ISBN: 978-0-7618-5594-1 (clothbound : alk. paper)
ISBN: 978-0-7618-5593-4 (paperback : alk. paper)
eISBN: 978-0-7618-5595-8

CONTENTS

TABLES AND FIGURES

TABLES:

FIGURES:

ACKNOWLEDGEMENTS

Sociology and much of the social sciences have neglected lean production as a major force in the economic and social division of labor. In the 1970s, Harry Braverman's book *Labor and Monopoly Capital* (1974) was widely read and cited in most sociological literature as declining skills and Fordism (i.e., the minute division of labor on the assembly line) were shown to affect the middle class and even the professions. But most of sociology misses this key aspect of lean production as a form of the division of labor, either assuming that lean production is more or less the same as Fordism, or that it affects too small a proportion of the workforce. But just as Taylorism or scientific management and Fordism directly impacted only about half of the workforce (i.e., not everyone worked on an assembly line), so the same applies to lean production. George Ritzer's *The McDonaldization of Society* (1993) has gotten large amount of attention in recent years, but McDonaldization is a variety of Fordism and scientific management with a little emotion work thrown in. Currently, hospitals are embracing lean production and not McDonaldization. The two work processes are not the same. While business, labor studies and journalism study lean production, sociology has largely ignored the direct study of lean production though Robert Cole is an early exception.

The fall of communism and globalization are two reasons why there is such neglect. Since Marxism as a political force embedded in the state has disappeared, sociologists give less credence to the impact of work on the masses. The working class is no longer a strategic actor on the world stage. Second, globalization focuses on the redistribution of work to China and India, and to the rather Fordist and poor working conditions there and in other developing countries. But with these changes in sociological and social science focus, the key to unlocking labor processes and conditions is being lost.

Our book is a partial attempt to refocus the sociological search light on the core processes of one of the most dynamic industries in the world, one on which consumers spend more money than any other product other than their houses or apartments. And within this larger view of the changing division of labor, we examine the impact on diversity, one key weakness in the continuing spread of lean production. We hope that our small effort contributes to a resurgence of research in this vital area of the labor process and division of labor.

In pursing this project, we have incurred many debts. We would like to thank the Presidents of Kaizen Motors and two of its suppliers, and especially the diversity officers and the members of the Human Resources Department who were instrumental in supporting this study and helping us gain *entrée*. This is an important event on their and our parts because very few social scientists have been fortunate enough to be able to conduct interviews inside a Japanese transplant. Even though we cannot mention the corporation or each person's name, we could not have done these interviews inside the plant on company time without their help and support. We would also like to thank Dr. Joachim Knuf for his valuable assistance throughout the study and Dr. Codrina Cozma for working closely with us on editing our manuscript at various stages. Professor Vicki Smith of the University of California at Davis assisted us with a number of issues related to temporary workers. At the University of Kentucky, Professor James Hougland gave us a number of insights into the workings of Japanese transplants, Professor Edward Morris advised us on difference theory, and we consulted Chrystal Henderson Grey on a number of different types of workers. Also from the University of Kentucky, Sarah Condley in computer support and Justin Conder in Sociology provided valuable assistance for the second author in formatting the text for final production. Dan Rust supplied contrasting information on American companies and Japanese transplants. The Beers Summer Graduate Fellowship provided helpful funding early in the project, and the CHSS Faculty Scholarship Award at Kennesaw State University supported later rewrites. We also thank Patricia E. White and Jan Stets at the National Science Foundation Grant for their help on "The Maturing of Lean Production" (NSF-ARRA 0940807) that provided summer support in the later stages of preparing this manuscript. Many thanks also go to all the colleagues in the Department of Sociology and Criminal Justice at Kennesaw State University who offered us their valuable support throughout the writing of this book. Finally, we would like to thank the over one hundred assembly line and paint shop workers who gave us their time and in many cases bared their hearts to us in our interviews.

Darina Lepadatu, Kennesaw   Thomas Janoski, Lexington

Chapter 1

BRINGING DIVERSITY TO TEAMS IN JAPANESE TRANSPLANTS

We are committed to forging innovative, diverse relationships with lasting, positive impact on our communities and our world. We believe these relationships make it possible for us to deliver excellence year-after-year.

Honda of America

By embracing diversity, we respect the uniqueness in background, experience, talent and personal characteristics in ourselves, our customers and our business partners. Diversity is about recognizing that different people have different perspectives, and that those differences can contribute to the good of an entire organization or company.   *Mitsubishi Motor Corporation of America*

As an international corporation, we're committed to diversity because we're committed to excellence. At Nissan in North America, diversity means opportunities for our entire workforce, respect for all individuals and inclusion of new ideas and viewpoints. Diversity strengthens us as individuals and as a company, better preparing us to create quality products.

Nissan Motor Corporation of North America

In the new millennium, the debate about the state of the auto industry has exploded on the national and international stage. Two of the three major American auto producers requested and received bailouts from the American government, while Japanese auto manufacturers were doing better in terms of sales and quality during the 2008-2010 economic down turn. Then Toyota and secondarily other auto companies were hit with major quality problems that put drivers' lives in jeopardy. After considerable public relations and financial damage, that controversy was more or less laid to rest. But despite the extensive media coverage, the Japanese auto manufacturers using lean production methods are on the rise and at the forefront of producing environmentally friendly hybrid and other high mileage cars. They also redoubled their lean approach to quality improvement. Since 2007, Toyota became and still is the number one auto maker in the world. And their principles of lean production have spread out into other industries from hospitals to insurance companies and universities (Chalice 2008, Grunden 2008, Graban 2009). The Japanese transplants are in the lead on sales and interest in the future development of the Japanese model is higher than ever. But there is one area in which Japanese transplants have stumbled.[1]

Japan is a very homogenous country where few women or minorities are employed in auto companies on a permanent basis. As the Japanese transplants passed from their start-up to the mature phase of production, major cultural and social tensions between American requirements for diversity and the Japanese model started to emerge. The quotes about diversity that open this chapter are now prominently displayed on the website of their North American operations, and this is partially because a number of law suits at Mitsubishi and Toyota over sexual harassment led to multi-million dollar settlements that have hurt and embarrassed the Japanese transplants and their managers. Thus, the real challenge for the Japanese transplants is diversity.

Diversity and teamwork are currently among the most important human resources strategies for boosting team performance and ultimately, organizational performance. Corporations spend millions of dollars on diversity programs, but the current research is still inconclusive about "how diversity works" in production teams in core industries. Consequently, we are looking at how one Japanese factory deals with diversity and at the same time maintains a high level of production and quality in a teamwork setting. More specifically, we examine how diverse Americans—women, African-Americans, older and younger workers— work together in lean production teams.

Teamwork is critical to the success of Japanese transplant organizations and to the manner in which diversity is brought into the workplace. This book shows how diversity works for employees on the shop floor of a Japanese factory located in America that we shall call Kaizen Motors. Further, this study demonstrates how some workers form strong bonds with team members, ties that are sometimes stronger than among friends and family. Worker identities are reshaped by their experiences at Kaizen Motors, sometimes with rather surprising results. For instance, many women feel empowered by their experiences at work, and this affects their presentation of self as attractive women. Thus, we uncover the tensions, emotions, challenges, and even joys of a diverse workforce cooperating, laboring, and dealing within highly intense team situations.

This case study of diversity and group dynamics belongs to a research tradition in sociology on small groups. As Brooke Harrington and Gary Fine (2006; Silver 1997) point out, small groups have become a "unique arena where all the action is," meaning that the study of small groups allows sociologists to observe the rich detail of workers' challenges, disasters, and triumphs. The small group is also the crossroads of self and society, and its systematic study can unearth the changing identities of men/women, blacks/whites, old/young, and secure/temporary workers in different cultural and organizational contexts. High performance groups can develop their own micro-cultures of work and diversity, which may show how large numbers of other groups deal with diversity in the rest of society.

The initial focus of this study was to compare teams with different degrees of diversity and to reveal the conditions and circumstances that lead diverse teams to have a lower or higher performance than homogenous teams. In the end, the project offers a complex in-depth analysis of diversity at the team and group level focusing on the quality of intra-group relations—feeling valued and respected—and how individual identities impact group effectiveness. While most of the previous studies of diversity revealed how the diversity of opinions, abilities, skills and experience stimulates creativity and problem solving in project teams or top management teams, our goal has been to reveal how diversity works in a blue-collar environment.

This study is the first in-depth analysis of diversity in the context of high performance work systems in a major automotive plant. High performance work systems rely on extensive selection and training, teamwork, intensified work, decentralized decision-making, flexible jobs and open communication (Evans and Davis 2005; Appelbaum et al. 2000). Diversity should ideally have a tremendous impact on high performance work systems that are obsessed with quality and continuing improvement (Womack et al. 1990), but the contribution of diversity to the performance of lean systems has not yet been explored. A number of observational studies have revealed the basic start-up and initial lean production processes of Japanese transplants—NUMMI in Fremont, California (Adler 1992), Mazda in Flat Rock, Michigan (Fucini and Fucini 1995), Toyota in Georgetown, Kentucky (Besser 1996), Subaru-Isuzu in Indiana (Graham 1995), Nissan in Sunderland, England (Garrahan and Stewart 1992), two electronics transplants in UK (Delbridge 1998), and a GM-Suzuki joint venture in Ontario, Canada (Rinehart, Huxley and Robertson 1997). Although a couple of them have briefly touched the topic of gender and race in the car industry (Besser 1996; Graham 1995), our book brings a significant contribution to literature on the human side of auto transplants since we focus directly on the nature of work relationships across gender, race and age lines and its impact on the overall employee satisfaction and well-being.

The Maturing of Lean Production

The initial studies of lean production were mainly of the start-up phase. Any attention paid to diversity was applied to the hiring process and whether the members of various status groups could do the job. The main question was whether the Japanese lean production system could work in the US, and that question has been answered with a resounding "yes." But in the mature state of lean production, five developments have occurred. First, workers have settled-in after ten to twenty years on the job. Their own cultures—gendered, racial, aging, and security cultures—now come to the fore. Second, identities develop over time in organizational and status group contexts. Men and women age and develop different views of each other. Some workers have been promoted and others not. Some people find work satisfying and they have thrived, while others find work alienating and they have complained or quit. Team situations are especially infused with an informal group with particular norms and values. These may differ from group to group, but they constrain and encourage certain kinds of behaviors. Third, the lean production context has changed. The once rigorous selection process taking place over a month has been replaced by trial work periods lasting as long as four years. These temporary workers are hired at lower pay and fewer benefits to do exactly the same work. Then after a few months or a few years, they are hired or let go. The introduction of temporary workers represents a reserve army of employees to remind the permanent workers that they can be easily replaced. As a result, workers may be in conflict with management and each other. Fourth, teamwork, quality programs, and suggestion systems have largely run their course and have tended to fade for some teams. And fifth, since many workers were hired at the same time, a large number of them are now bottled up at the entry gates of promotion.

The end result is a complex mixture of incentives, feelings, and day-to-day realities. Workers in the transplants have worked with mandatory overtime for some years. Some workers have done well, and others have just survived. Thus, the context of "mature lean production" is leaner and relentless leaving some workers fatigued and other workers exhilarated and re-shaped.

Problems with Team Diversity Theory

After more than forty years of initiatives and policies promoting diversity at work, this continues to be one of the most controversial debates in the field of organizations. The findings of thirty different research studies on the link between diversity and team performance that we examined are contradictory: "Organizational diversity is a slippery construct" (Ragins and Gonzalez 2003), "diversity is a double-edged sword" (Milliken and Martins 1996; Ragins and Gonzalez 2003), and "dealing with diversity is like opening Pandora's box" (Shapiro 2000). The impact of diversity on team performance can be positive, curvilinear or negative (Harrison et al. 2002; Lau and Murnigham 1998). Others find that understanding diversity is difficult (Simsarian et al. 2001), and that "much is still unknown about the relationship between diversity and team performance" (Pelled et al.1999). On the impact of diversity on performance, one major study indicates that "conclusive findings still do not exist" and "the relationship is obviously not straightforward and might have been overstated" (Simsarian et al. 2001).

In the field of team diversity, six problematic areas exist concerning how these studies have been done and their subsequent inclusion in meta-analyses. The first problem is that increased access of gender, age, racial and ethnic minorities to more workplaces makes completely homogenous organizations harder to find. Most workplaces already have or will soon employ a large degree of diversity. The question is no longer whether the heterogeneous teams work better than the homogenous teams, but how to deal with and capitalize on the potential of diverse teams. In this study, we are able to study teams that vary from being diverse to homogenous.

The second problem is that organizational diversity and organizational demography are sometimes seen as overlapping areas of research (Tsui and Gutek 1999). The diversity field often uses case studies, while the organizational demography approach focuses on the causes and consequences of group composition using compositional studies. A newer approach called relational demography promises to combine the two (Tsui et al. 1992; Ely 1994 1995; Ibarra 1995; Bacharach et al. 2005). All in all, a major problem of demographic research is that it assumes that these three types of research are equivalent (Tsui and Gutek 1999; Simsarian et al. 2001). But this study will clearly fall into the case study area with our interviews and some data coming from organizational surveys.

A third problem concerns the way in which one should balance the advantages and the disadvantages of diversity. Although the advantages of diversity are important (i.e., increased creativity, high quality ideas, suggestions, and objectivity), there are some downsides to diversity that must be considered with teams (i.e., increased conflict, less commitment and cohesion, and longer time needed to reach a decision) (Simsarian et al. 2001; Milliken and Martins 1996; Williams and O'Reilly 1998; Kirkman et al. 2004). Researchers warn that increasing demographic variation does not automatically lead to an increase in organizational effectiveness. Thomas and Ely (1996) indicate that it is "how a company defines diversity" and uses the "experiences of being a diverse organization" that makes diversity work or not.

Fourth, the debate becomes more complicated when the differences between managed and unmanaged diversity are considered. The relationship between team diversity and performance will clearly differ if it is carefully managed or simply neglected. Some firms use explicit and sometimes well designed diversity policies, but other firms have teams with no stated diversity policy at all. Clearly, the relationship between team diversity and team performance will vary when management implements a clearly focused policy or when management ignores the issue of diversity and just hopes for the best. Particularly important in this area are team training programs for diversity. While previous meta-analysis studies on work teams have always differentiated diversity and performance results based on managed and unmanaged diversity, this study will clearly be a carefully managed study.

Fifth, diversity is not a holistic concept. Findings can be contradictory because different types of diversity impact team performance in different ways, but again there is little consensus in the literature concerning which types of diversity work best. Are the most visible attributes—gender, age and race—the most important (Williams and O'Reilly 1998), or are the more job-related attributes—formal education, work experience, employment status, specific knowledge, individual skills and abilities—more effective (Milliken and Martins 1996)? This study will show how these two types of diversity interact, especially with gender and age.

Further, the nature of diversity varies with different types of teams. It is commonly assumed that teams in high-skilled jobs or project teams can benefit more from diversity than teams in low-skilled jobs. It is often implied that teams in low-skilled jobs cannot directly benefit from the traditional advantages of diversity—creativity, free-thinking, objectivity, innovation. Instead, they may be ravaged by the disadvantages of diversity—conflict, inconsistency, and low commitment. The research on diverse teams is abundant on studies on top-management teams, but little research exists on shop floor teams. Researchers have neglected the effects of diversity on production teams or in blue collar jobs, and this is exactly what we are trying to explore in this book.

Sixth and finally, the problems of previous meta-analyses lead to the dilemma of laboratory versus field findings. Most of the studies on team diversity that are optimistic about the beneficial role of ascriptive attributes—gender, age, race and ethnicity—on team performance are experimental studies on ad-hoc teams of college students. Existing studies on permanent work groups are less optimistic about the effect of diversity on group outcomes (Pelled 1996; Tsui et al. 1992). Because student teams have a very limited life cycle which does not allow the team members to bond or to even have conflicts, more research on real work teams in real working environments is needed. This study on Kaizen Motors addresses many of these issues by focusing on managed-diversity in lean production teams that actually exist in day-to-day production on the shop-floor.

A Theory of Team Intensification

Our theoretical perspective integrates elements of the symbolic interactionist theory—building on the concepts of multiple generalized others and positive emotions—and the revised contact hypothesis in teams with high levels of interaction (Pettigrew and Tropp 2006; Allport 1954). We also incorporate some aspects of the cultural diversity perspective (Ely and Thomas 2001) and organizational theories of tokenism (Kanter 1977b), but in a more contingent manner.

Symbolic interactionism provides the basis for understanding the identities of one's self and others (Mead 1964, 1967; Blumer 1969; Goffman 1959, 1963; Scheff 2003). George Herbert Mead's theory of symbolic interactionism uses the "I," the "me," and the "generalized other" to form the "self" in relation to the broader context of society. For Mead, the generalized other is a community of attitudes reflected back upon the "me," and the "I" responds by creating or adjusting the self. The 'me' presents the self, and it often represents the socialized, predictable, controlled aspect of the self. The "I" represents the creative and directive part of the self. The "generalized other" is the key mechanism in Mead's theory that consists of the attitudes of others as they view someone as being similar or different (Mead 1967). But there are often multiple generalized others that exist in a hierarchy of importance (Janoski, Grey and Lepadatu 2007, 2010a, 2010b). For example, a worker may have different generalized others based on gender, race, team affiliation, family, neighbourhood or political views. The discussion of difference and identity must begin from relating and often ranking these generalized others or "how others see you."

The formation of the generalized other in a team context is a complex process. The members of diverse teams may start out viewing their team members as generalized others representing various race, age, and gender groups. Teams bond when a clear generalized other forms upon the team and its members, and a woman or African-American is viewed first and foremost as a member of that team. When a team member says "they," the meaning derives from the team status, not gender or racial status. Intergroup contact combined with open interaction in a successful group changes one's "generalized other" from being based on ascriptive characteristics to being focused on full membership in a team and an overall corporate group. Further, this transformation of "your group" to "my team" involves positive emotions focused on the important contributions of team mates.

Secondly, we embed the "revised contact hypothesis" into team intensification theory, and connect this to diversity theory in organizations (Pettigrew and Tropp 2006; Wright and Richard 2010; Dovidio et al. 2005; Jones 2002; Pettigrew 1998; Allport 1954). The more sophisticated contact hypothesis includes four elements: (1) contact between people of equal status who are perceived to be different, (2) joint participation in linked tasks preferably in a small group (i.e. a 'team'), (3) legitimacy of working in a diverse environment expressed by leaders respected by both groups, and (4) a successful outcome recognized by both groups. While the initial contact hypothesis faltered because simple contact can produce conflict, the revised contact hypothesis has worked well in reducing discrimination and negative attitudes toward other groups. The weakness of the revised contact hypothesis lies in the difficulties of getting people of diverse races or genders to work together on a project when widespread residential or occupational segregation exists. And many policy interventions are based on this more diffuse approach (Jones 2002:176-188). Ironically, this weakness becomes a strength in the lean production environment. Most work is organized into teams (point 2), and management is highly supportive of both diverse teams (point 3) and successful outcomes – building a high quality automobile at a reasonable cost (point 4). Of the three approaches that focus on how contact changes attitudes, the "recategorization model" with a new "in-group identity" describes Kaizen Motors quite well (Gaertner et al. 1990, 1994, 2005). The revised contact hypothesis clearly fits what diversity research refers to as "managed diversity." This is the mechanism by which diversity improves performance through social interaction.[2]

But we push contact theory into a more specific team intensification perspective where there are more consequences to long and high-pressured hours at work. Other things happen in addition to the constant contact between team members of equal status participating together in successful teams with the diversity being legitimated by management. With mandatory overtime working 60 or more hours a week, team members see less and less of their families, especially their spouses. In many teams (but not those with temporary workers), workers become more and more attached to their team members. Attachment leads to emotional and physical attraction, and sometimes dating, divorce, and then marriage within the team environment. While company policy assigns spouses to different teams, it is clear that team intensity goes beyond diversity and cooperation to emotional relationships that can leave a wake of fractured families.

Another aspect of team intensification is that those women and ethnic minorities who thrive in the team environment have a major boost in positive identity. Some women, though clearly dealing with a difficult work environment, lose weight and become more attractive. By doing a tough job well, their confidence rises, and their incomes are higher than many of the men in their neighborhoods and family of origin. Some African Americans, while dealing with tough work and minority status, do well in terms of getting promotions to team and group leaders. In their communities, both women and African-American team members have high status for having survived the work but also for belonging to a corporation that "does it right, as one African-American worker put it. In some cases, they develop positive self-images based on the feedback from their team "generalized other" that instills a greater confidence than one might expect.

Thus, team intensification theory begins with the revised contact hypothesis in a very specialized and intense setting, but the processes and consequences go beyond the desired outcome of diverse people getting along. One must keep in mind two contrary outcomes. First, there are women and minorities (and white men for that matter) who are either dismissed from work or quit this intense environment. But this reinforces the identity and pride of those who are successful. And secondly, the use of temps totally violates team intensification theory with workers doing the same work and getting lesser rewards.

Two other theories that we thought would have a stronger effect only worked in some situations. Rosabeth Kanter's (1977a, b) groundbreaking research on the importance of numbers and ratios on social interaction analyzes the experiences of women and African-Americans in token status (less than 15% of the workforce) in a large corporation. Her research emphasizes the psychosocial difficulties that team members with token status face in workplace. These difficulties range from fear of visibility, performance pressures, exaggeration of differences and dominant culture to role encapsulation and boundary heightening. Tokens also tend to isolate themselves and dissociate from one another because of the pressures that they experience from the dominant group, thus reinforcing the self-perpetuating vicious cycle of tokenism. Kanter (1977b) advocates intervention to break the cycle created by the social composition of group. She paves the way for a growing body of research on the significance of proportions in the social life of groups. We apply Kanter's perspective on tokenism to explain group functioning and social interaction in groups with low, medium and high diversity, but find that it applies to only a few situations but not to most, and in some surprising cases, it operates in the opposite direction.

Lastly, Robin Ely and Richard Thomas (2001) delineate three strategies toward diversity that managers use. Most of the companies use the access-and-legitimacy perspective (where diversity is incorporated for facilitating access to minority markets but not incorporated into core functions) or the discrimination-and-fairness perspective (where diversity is encouraged within the company as to ensure a fair treatment to all employees). Only the integration-and-learning perspective provides the rationale and guidance needed to achieve sustained benefits from diversity. This perspective says that the insights, skills and experiences that employees have developed as members of various cultural identity groups are valuable resources that the work group can use to rethink its primary tasks. We find that this approach of each group's special knowledge advancing the company has a small amount of informal applicability to women and older workers but not to African-Americans and others. Women and minorities might have an advantage in selling cars to diverse customers, but they do not seem to have any major advantage in making cars.

Thus, our team intensification theory combines the symbolic interactionist theory of identity and the "other" with the revised contact hypothesis in a special setting where teams have very high levels of interaction. We incorporate some contingent effects of Ely and Thomas' integration and learning perspective and Kanter's numbers theory, but find the application of these theories that are so effective in other venues are only partially effective here.[3] In the end, constant contact in teams has solidaristic effects that benefit production and work groups, and also have unintended effects, both positive and negative, that go beyond the team environment.[4]

Teamwork and Diversity in Japanese Transplants

The dynamics of diversity in a Japanese factory are intimately linked with the nature of interpersonal relations in teams. The next two sections look at these two processes in Japanese transplants.

Teamwork. From the perspective of the sociology of work, the significance of lean production (also called *Toyotism* or the Toyota system of production) lies in its teamwork, worker involvement, direct participation, and continuous training for all workers. It also requires deep commitment from both managers and employees in order to detect any flaw in production and to eliminate waste. The result is an increasing level of quality over time that will eliminate the need for inspection and rework. Other important aspects of *Toyotism* include welfare corporatism, job security, organizational culture, and consensus decision-making (Besser 1996). The so-called Japanese miracle, besides the technical factors, is also based on a more thorough inclusion of the social (cultural, ideological, normative) dimension of work on the line. Most of the workers' needs or suggestions will be answered by Human Resources Departments that take care of workers' welfare. Bonuses, day care, picnics, concerts, training and college classes are only some of the initiatives organized by lean companies for strengthening the "community of faith" with their workers (Besser 1996).

There are many positive aspects of working in teams—greater job satisfaction, creativity, commitment, autonomy, meaning in work, job security, and cooperation (Batt and Appelbaum 1995). Paul Adler finds that teams not only generate a sense of commitment and loyalty, but they become mini-labs of spontaneous learning transforming the organizations in "learning bureaucracies" (1992). They also have faster reactivity and flexibility regarding unforeseen circumstances that happen on the line. Ideally, teams should react faster to change and solve problems better than in the traditional Fordist system that is not based on a team concept. Teamwork also improves productivity, quality, attendance, adaptability and flexibility, especially in accepting and creating innovations.

But teams have a downside with time consuming decision-making processes, increased peer pressure, and sometimes increased conflict among people (Simsarian-Webber and Donahue 2001; Ragins and Gonzalez 2003; Milliken and Martins 1996; Williams and O'Reilly 1998). For instance, the Toyota Corporation is open about the fact that employees undertake enormous responsibilities in the Toyota Production System. The company warns that the broad-range of responsibilities workers have to deal with at Toyota may come as a shock for those who are used with rigid job designations. Time pressure and empowerment are rigorously mentioned throughout the corporate information booklet and in their information seminars (Toyota 1998; Toyota 2004; also Nissan 2009)

Many of the early studies of lean production are optimistic about the social invention of lean production, especially James Womack, Daniel Jones and Daniel Roos' (1990) influential volume but also others (Kenney and Florida 1993; Cole 1985). Later analyses became more critical (Adler 1992, Fucini and Fucini 1995, Besser 1996, Graham 1995, Garrahan and Stewart 1992, Delbridge 1998, and Rinehart, Huxley and Robertson 1997). Some of these later studies describe the lean system of production as "management by stress" (Parker and Slaughter 1988), as indoctrination that is "so effective that the workers do not even know how miserable they are" (Garrahan and Stewart 1992), or as a system that "makes you feel like having a hundred bosses instead of one" (Besser 1996).

Teams can be manipulated by management to encourage employees to monitor each other and report to management (Delbridge 1998). Work intensification, increased injury rates and even unkind acts toward team members have all been reported in team settings (Graham 1995). An extreme expression of the discontent with the lean system of production took place in 1992, when the CAMI plant in Canada experienced the first strike in a lean auto factory—"the strike that was not supposed to happen." Workers burned company T-shirts and carried banners that crossed out the company slogans of "open communication, empowerment, *kaizen*, and team spirit" and replaced them with "dignity, respect, fairness, and solidarity." The majority of the workers interviewed by researchers said that they are doing too much work with too few people, especially when team members are absent or injured. Most managers actually agreed that workers at the CAMI plant work harder than workers in other plants (Rinehart et al. 1997).

Many researchers observe that beyond the high-paced work on the assembly line in the auto industry, the lean production system imposes more stress. Just-in-time production, continuous improvement, mandatory overtime, and even empowerment frequently create greater anxiety, fears of falling behind, and peer pressure. In the long run, these stresses affect the overall well-being of workers. As their physical and mental health is under assault, their work performance, family life, and even attempts at recreation may suffer. Nonetheless, Japanese management in American transplants have built their prestige and success on recognizing the value of their human resources equally with their technological innovations. Despite the stress, the balance of human and technological factors still differentiates the Japanese model from the traditional Fordist organization system.

The Japanese system of lean production does not involve a new form of worker democracy as is sometimes claimed. According to Hans Pruijt (2003), teamwork in the lean system fails to live up to its expectations of democracy and equity simply because lean manufacturing is not an anti-Taylorist system like the Swedish and German systems.[5] Toyotism can be considered a neo-Tayloristic system of production because it keeps the most central ideas of Taylorism intact, especially technical improvement in assembly line production (Pruijt 2003; Dohse et al. 1985). The difference is that workers now join engineers in pursuing improved production. The early work of Taiichi Ono, the father of the Toyota production system, surprisingly does not include any references of teamwork. Instead, "Team Toyota" refers to workers' responsibility for the whole enterprise.

In comparison with the socio-technical or group work approaches, teams in the lean production system have limited empowerment. Team leaders as supervisors are not democratically elected by team members, and various participatory forums do not exist as in socio-technical approaches. Further, when team leaders are selected, they are often assigned to new team assignments, not to their original teams. In the *Toyotism* system, *takt* (job cycle) time is decided two levels up in the hierarchy, and the worker's discretion for using the *andon* cord that stops the line is mainly for decreasing defects. The team member does not have much discretion in the way they organize their own work. In the Swedish systems, there were instances when workers wanted even to abolish the assembly-line or they modified it to increase worker autonomy (Pruijt 2003; Berggren 1993). But Pruijt does admit that while lean production is "not a stunning triumph of organizational democracy," it does have "at least some examples of worker control" (2003).

On the same lines, Vicki Smith (1997) criticizes new organizational forms including quality circles, job rotation, continuous improvement, organizational decentralization, and just-in-time inventory procedures. She finds that flexible forms of production do not bring a break with traditional hierarchical modes of control and authority relations, but "embody and even deepen authority and control by obscuring power behind participatory language" (Smith 1997: 316). In the lean systems, workers are less controlled by their supervisors, and more controlled by technology, their own peers, and sometimes even customers. Despite trying to avoid the ills of mass production (e.g., dissatisfaction, boredom, alienation, high absenteeism, and turnover), lean production is a more subtle system of normative control.

Others support both Pruijt and Smith in their view of team-based production as being more de-centered and relying on less visible tactics of control. Yates and co-authors (2001) criticize it for being the "Trojan horses of empowerment," Barker (1993) calls it tightening the "iron cage," Sinclair (1992) asserts that it instigates a tyranny of team ideology, Sewell (1998) sees it as disciplining through surveillance (Sewell 1998), Vallas (2003, 2006) notes the limits of teamwork, and Ezzamel and Willmot (1998) conclude that it is threatening workers' self-identities. Lean production and Toyotism do introduce more worker participation than Fordism, but certainly much less the socio-technical or group work approaches.[6] Consequently, one should neither overstate the participatory elements nor understate the stresses and strains of the lean system.

Although teamwork in lean production intends a moderate amount of equity, it ironically generates more inequality through intentional wage and security discrimination. Companies using lean production often hire a significant number of temporary workers as a buffering strategy. These "temps" have no job security, lower wages, fewer benefits, and are not even recognized by the company as their own employees because they are actually employed by subcontracting temporary work agencies such as Manpower. The wage inequality between the temporary and the permanent workers can induce tensions and resentments between the members of the same team. This often overlooked division between core and peripheral workers festers within teams, and needs to be addressed.

The history of recruitment also leads to employee conflict because the demographic age structure of the workforce is largely determined by the hiring of large cohorts at once in the 1980s. With low rates of turnover and secure long-term employment, teams are dominated by workers in their forties or fifties with high wages. Meanwhile, the small numbers of younger workers are more likely to be composed of temporary workers with lower wages.

Teams in the lean system of production generally have about five members with sometimes as many as ten members.[7] The size of the teams is generally dictated by the nature of the production system, but lean production tends to keep teams below ten and closer to five workers. Since team leaders can only make quick responses when teams are small, lean teams need to be small in the range of five to eight workers.

Diversity. From the very beginning, the hiring practices of the Japanese auto transplants were under tight scrutiny in the US. Japan's population is much more homogenous than the US with very little immigration, and only 55% of Japanese women in the workforce. When they do go to work, Japanese women tend to be "office ladies" or teachers (Ogasawara 1998; Mehri 2005; Aoki et al. 2008). This cannot be the case of a Japanese company in the US. The Mazda plant in Flat Rock was the first Japanese transplant in America when it opened in Michigan. Although Mazda managers avoid hiring female production workers in Japan, they knew that they would have to accept women in the US. For the most part, the Japanese managers and trainers were totally inexperienced with female workers.

One of the first challenges faced by American women in Japanese trans-plants was the contrast between the traditional notion of femininity in Japan versus in the US and the nature of their work on the assembly line. The Ameri-can women faced the Japanese view that they are inherently weaker, less capa-ble than men and that they needed to be closely watched. Some Japanese man-agers at the Mazda plant initially had the impression that women who work in a male-dominated factory must be sexually loose but this was immediately cor-rected by upper management (Fucini and Fucini 1990). When Mazda offered classes on Japanese culture, half of those learning samurai sword drills were women, and half of those arranging flowers and conducting tea ceremonies were men. More generally, the Japanese managers were surprised by the assertiveness of the American women.

At least in the start-up phase, many Japanese managers treated women un-fairly. At first, many trainers pushed women around more than men and screamed at them more harshly (Fucini and Fucini 1990: 112). During the train-ing courses, women were addressed in a sarcastic way if they did not immedi-ately catch on to a lesson, and the trainers clearly preferred to teach the Ameri-can male workers first, and then asked the American men to teach the women. Eventually, the Japanese trainers became accustomed with the American gender norms, and the harassment and intimidation stopped. Women even started to appreciate working at the Mazda plant, and one states that "If a woman walked through the plant at Ford it was like a zoo" but at Mazda "It's not like that at all here" (Fucini and Fucini 1990: 62).[8]

The Japanese managers had little sympathy for the sometimes conflicting demands of job and family because men did not have a role in managing day-to-day family affairs in Japan. Judy, a single mother of two teenage kids, asked for the manager's permission to go to a doctor's appointment, and he told her that she would be punished if she takes care of personal problems during company time (Fucini and Fucini 1990: 115). She left anyway and was reprimanded. Women were disappointed about the Japanese manager's lack of understanding of family roles in the US, and also said that they "know women who've had kids sick at home, and they couldn't get permission to use the phone for five minutes to call them" (1990: 115).

In the first phase, most of the Japanese transplants had been located in rural and somewhat disadvantaged regions that happened to be largely white areas of the South (Kentucky, Tennessee, and Alabama) or in low income areas of the Midwest (Ohio, Illinois, and Indiana). Only one plant was situated in a traditional auto manufacturing area (Mazda in Michigan). This raised the concerns of the black community since it previously had access to jobs in the auto industry. For instance, since their start-up, Honda factories had been accused of denying employment opportunities to African-Americans by using a hiring radius requirement. The Honda Civic plant in Greensburg accepts workers from only 20 out of 79 Indiana counties, counties that happen to be 96% white (Bybee 2008). Most of the African-American workers at the Mazda plant describe their relationship with the Asian managers as being OK, which means that they do not bother each other, but they do not have close relationships or socialize outside work (Fucini and Fucini 1990).[9]

At Subaru-Isuzu in Indiana, Laurie Graham (1995) found that women and African-Americans faced discrimination. Women got the lower-paying and the hardest jobs, their physical abilities were often questioned, and their leadership potential was ignored. Women were also asked more often to do the sweeping and the cleaning after work. The burden of overtime is more intense for women because of their psychological as well as physical responsibilities in the home. As an insider who worked on the line at Subaru-Isuzu, Graham describes that there was a wide perception at the plant that carpal tunnel syndrome is a "woman disease." In an attempt to break down these rumors, women would rarely go to see the doctor, and preferred to suffer in silence. Graham's point is that women experience the intensification of work differently than men because of their role in the family. There were no African-Americans in management positions above team leader because Subaru-Isuzu, according to Graham, did not want to hire unionists and they viewed black workers as pro-union. Thus, the screening procedures filtered out many black applicants.

At the CAMI plant in Canada, which is a Suzuki-GM joint venture, Rinehart, Huxley and Robertson (1997) noticed some tensions over gender relations. Some men felt that women got easier jobs with better working conditions, such as paint and subassembly (rather than stamping and welding). But surveys showed that three-quarters of male and female respondents thought that they were treated equally. Younger males were reportedly more open to work side by side with women. One woman reports that male co-workers did not always know how to act: "Some feel like they should always help a woman; others stand back and let me see if I can do it" (1997:114). One female manager wanted more women to go into non-traditional jobs, but she said that women do not like welding because "it's dirtier, noisy and hard work to do" and they are "intimidated" by the robots and sparks (1997:115). But the CAMI study found that women have twice as many repetitive strain injuries than men, and that a majority of women said that they were tired "all the time" or "often" because of their second shift of housework.[10]

Regarding diversity and teamwork, the CAMI study concludes that team-work can aggravate the nature of the relations between men and women in de-manding jobs. As a local union leader put it, men are frustrated by working with women in teams because women could not pick up the slack and men had to do extra work. Men did not want women on their teams because in the job rotation cycle, women would more frequently take the easier jobs and men would end up with the harder ones. A male team member complains that women do not install back seats as part of their job rotation but he is "sure as hell" not going to do it himself because he is too old for this type of work (Rinehart et al. 1997:118). As a solution to this problem, two persons were assigned to install the back seats. In other plants, they introduced come-along seats that made this much easier. So what seemed to be a gender problem became a job design problem.

The overlap between gender concerns and team pressure was even more evident after workers came back from a medical leave related to an injury. In-jured workers could not refuse to do the jobs that had injured them as part of the job rotation. When they could not rotate onto those jobs, there was so much pressure from the other team members that they went on medical leave for stress. Under the Canadian Human Rights Code, the workers and the union filed a complaint blaming CAMI's team concepts for "pitting worker against worker" (Rinehart et al. 1997:119). Teamwork, despite its many advantages, can alienate workers from each other and can bring enhanced pressure or inequity across gender or racial lines. The CAMI study concluded that lean production may af-fect women more severely than men because intra-team pressures exacerbate tensions across gender lines.

However, the bottom line for the Japanese transplants is that gender and ra-cial discrimination can be very expensive. In 1996 at the Mitsubishi plant in Illinois, 500 of 893 women filed a sexual discrimination lawsuit, claiming that they were victims of unwanted groping, grabbing, touching, and threats of job loss if they refused sexual favors. Further, when they complained, they suffered sexual comments and graffiti sometimes naming specific women. Ten African-American workers also charged the company for racial discrimination. Mitsubi-shi lawyers even argued in court that some women who had abortions were sexually loose. The local union did nothing to support the women's cause. Mit-subishi settled the $190,000,000 case out of court paying an undisclosed sum (claimed to be between $15,000,000 and $34,000,000), and had to establish di-versity programs and a diversity commission headed by former Secretary of Labor Alexis Herman to monitor conditions at their plants (*New York Times* 1999, Lattman 2006). At Toyota, a Japanese national resigned as President of Toyota Motor Manufacturing North American upon allegations that he made sexual advances to his Japanese female assistant. Toyota settled this case of $150,000,000 in damages for an undisclosed amount (*New York Times* 2006).[11] Clearly, gender and racial discrimination can be very expensive. Consequently, what happens at the team level can be critical to the financial position of the corporation.

Research Design: Explaining What Happens with Diversity in Teams

Our research design focuses on explaining the *degree of diversity* in a Japanese transplant. We obtained a range of teams based on diversity, teams and groups were divided into low (below 25%), medium (25-50%) and high diversity (more than 50% diversity) based on gender, race, age, and employment status. The focus is on perceived *team performance* (problem-solving, productivity, quality and safety) and *team functioning* (team morale, conflicts, emotions, and team member interactions).

This diversity research is qualitative because it is focused on the experiences of diversity. We used semi-structured interviews to penetrate the intimate life of teams, which can help us understand why low, moderate or high diversity teams work differently. They uncover more about the spirit of cooperation, climate, environment and identity of teams. The main portion of the in-depth interviews were done in the plant by the first author with 87 workers on 16 different teams selected on the basis of low, moderate, and high diversity. These production teams were also selected equally from both the first and second shifts. We then met with and interviewed managers in diversity, human resources and corporate affairs about diversity programs and other programs. This was followed by interviews by both authors with 55 additional employees (supplier workers and former workers at Kaizen Motors) about a range of issues from diversity to work stress.

We also used Kaizen Motors corporate reports on diversity and teamwork, and their annual surveys of employee opinion (see Appendix 2). These surveys reached all the workers in the plant and give us summary measures for women, men, African-Americans, temporary workers, and older/younger workers.[12] These opinion survey results were analyzed from computer files at Kaizen Motor. As a result, we analyzed 142 in-depth and over 3,000 survey interviews for this study. We also interviewed workers at one other Japanese transplant and two American auto companies. Thus, we obtained the workers' views in qualitative interviews, the managers' views in meetings and interviews, and we used the data that originated from corporate reports and employee opinion surveys.

Conclusion

We emphasize five major findings. First, moderately heterogeneous teams generally performed better than highly heterogeneous or homogenous teams. Moderately diverse teams performed better because they have a larger pool of ideas, skills and abilities that could be fashioned into productive advances. Second, team members from diverse groups altered their views of generalized others from a global "us and them" approach, and adopted team and 'group' generalized others. Third, white male team members will develop positive emotions toward diverse team members' contribution to the team based on working together and success. These positive emotions may range from humor to a more humane or interesting work environment due to differing points of view. Women's contribution to teams is often based on their different perspectives and more caring attitudes toward team members. Work in teams with women is more pleasant and enjoyable. But fourth, the lack of diversity concerning age between shifts can lead to conflicts between shifts and less productivity concerning these much larger groups. And fifth, teams with temporary workers have poor intergroup relations and low performance because they violate the equality of status requirement of the team intensification theory.

Teamwork in the context of Japanese management is a complex concept full of contradictions (Osono et al. 2008). It combines the benefits of empowerment with enhanced control, participation with peer pressure, job enrichment with work intensification. Similarly, diversity can also become a double-edge sword. The Japanese transplants do not have the best record on promoting equal opportunities at work or in combating sexual and racial harassment. Therefore, teams as the basic units of the Japanese auto factories are ideal places for observing how diversity operates on the shop floor.

Thirty years after the Japanese auto makers laid ground in the US, Honda, Nissan and Toyota are dominating the US and global auto markets. We are trying to understand how teamwork and diversity in Japanese transplants contribute to overall organizational success and performance. In the next chapters, we will analyze diversity and teamwork along four main dimensions: gender, race and ethnicity, age and employment status. Chapter 2 introduces the reader to Kaizen Motors and how it contextualizes teamwork and diversity. Chapter 3 looks at the surprising position of women at Kaizen Motors, whom we refer to as "the queens of the line." Chapter 4 discusses the dating, affairs and divorce at Kaizen Motors. Chapter 5 examines the wary position of African-Americans at Kaizen Motors where there is success and ambiguity. Chapter 6 sheds light on the "aging gurus" and the "young gung-hoes" and the respectful manner in which they interact within and between shifts. And Chapter 7 uncovers the "underdogs of the line," which constitute the most problematic group of workers at Kaizen because they are paid much less and have no job security.

Chapter 2

WELCOME TO KAIZEN MOTORS!

> The Kaizen vision is to be a respected company that produces the highest quality vehicles at the lowest cost in a safe environment. To ensure the success of our company, each team member has the responsibility to work together, communicate honestly, share ideas, and ensure teamwork throughout our corporation.
>
> Paraphrasing a statement in *The Kaizen Employees Handbook*

Kaizen Motors is an automotive assembly plant of a Fortune 500 corporation located east of the Mississippi River with about 4,000 to 11,000 employees. It was built on a green field site in a state east of the Mississippi River between 1980 and 2000. Since then it has produced high quality automobiles and vans that the American public has bought in large numbers. In its start-up phase, it was similar to most other Japanese automotive transplants with the organization using thousands of Japanese employees to guide the new American employees in its beginning phases, and about a quarter of its early employees took trips to Japan to see how their plants operated. With a few exceptions, most of the workers hired were not from the American automobile industry, and it sometimes appeared that the ideal worker came from the American fast food industry like McDonalds or Subway. Most employees came from a vast diversity of backgrounds with about forty-percent coming from rural areas. Some workers still commute long distances from urban or rural areas, but many of them who stayed at Kaizen gravitated to residences in nearby towns and small cities. All in all, its wages are higher than most jobs for blue-collar workers in the area, but they are slightly lower than the American auto plants. Over a period of five years, the hiring policy was changed to hiring temporary workers who then

would become permanent at some indefinite time in the future if they worked
out.

At the time of our study, the plant was still relatively new and it has been
expanded a number of times. As with most plants built within the last three dec-
ades, there was an extensive competition between five to ten states to offer land,
tax abatements, training subsidies, and other inducements to come to each competing state. Kaizen Motors went with the state that seemed to offer the most
advantageous package. It is located within ten miles of major roadways and rail
lines, which makes sense for a large industrial plant. Each aisle is rather large to
permit the movement of motorized equipment throughout the plant. A typical
feature of Japanese transplants are the *andon* boards that hang from the ceiling
and light up with codes to indicate problems in particular areas in the plant. As
indicated by MBWA or "management by walking around," managers and workers can look down each aisle of the plant and see if there are any pressing problems in at any particular moment. The plant also displays a number of banners
indicating awards that they have recently won.

Entrée and Confidentiality in a Case Study

Gaining entry into the plant was the most difficult and time consuming
phase of the project, and it lasted almost two years. After we obtained the official approval for the study from the company, a series of preliminary sessions
with corporate specialists at the plant followed in the next months. During these
meetings, we narrowed down the project to what is feasible to achieve taking
into consideration the data available from Kaizen, production cycles, time
frames, and so forth. Participation in this research project meant an equal enormous volume of work from the part of Kaizen Motor's diversity specialists, because they had to prepare many internal information memos and meetings to
communicate the purpose of the project throughout the plant. According to the
Japanese philosophy of decision-making, any approval process is preceded by
nemawashi, a preliminary process to involve other sections/departments in discussions to seek input, information and/or support for a proposal or change that
would affect them.

A large part of the delay occurred while the company's legal team reviewed
the project proposal. They prepared an agreement that we signed indicating that
we would not reveal the name of the company. As a result, we named the company Kaizen Motors after the term for "continuous improvement" and have had
to disguise the company's identifiable details, so that it will not be clear which
of the Japanese transplants we are studying. This is a common practice in sociology with similar pseudonyms of INDSCO (Kanter 1979) and ChemCo (Bond
2008) in case studies of diversity. As a result, the reader will notice that the description that we have just given is somewhat vague (e.g., a plant with "2,000 to
11,000 employees . . . built . . . between 1980 and 2000" could almost be any
Japanese transplant). It is somewhat frustrating not to be able to furnish some of
the details describing the plant in "color commentary," but that is balanced by

the fact that it is extremely rare for sociologists to obtain *entrée* into a Japanese transplant to interview workers about a sensitive topic. The company also assigned two contact persons from each shift who agreed to provide assistance with the project, and workers came off the line for interviews in a break room.

An organizational case study is the exploration of an organization over time through detailed, in-depth data collection involving multiple sources of information rich in context (Creswell, 1998). The multiple sources of information include observations, interviews, audio-visual material, documents and reports. The case being studied has to be bounded by time and place. The context (the physical setting, the social, historical or the economic setting) is crucial for the case study. Therefore, a case study approach best serves the purposes of our study, since it seeks to explore diversity as a working experience, not just as an increase in the demographic composition of teams. There are three types of case studies: intrinsic case studies that study the uniqueness of a particular case, instrumental case studies that study an issue within the case (diversity in a Japanese transplant in our case), and collective case studies that study multiple cases (Creswell, 1998). The advantage of using a case study is that the hypotheses can be adjusted continuously once the researcher gets more details from the field.

Although case studies had been traditionally considered qualitative studies *sui generis*, some social scientists do not find all case studies to be qualitative (Ragin and Becker, 1992). Further, Robert Stake (2000) does not see case studies as a method of inquiry, but rather as a study with an interest in individual cases. However, the intention here is to provide a case study that sheds light on what goes on in many different Japanese transplants. In this sense, it is similar to the logic expressed in Michael Burawoy's ethnography of a machine shop (1979) that indicates that the study of one plant gives information about what happens more generally in many different companies. Richard Yin (1994) includes both qualitative and quantitative methods in the case study development, and this is the approach that we take in this study. Thus, this is a case study that uses an array of qualitative and quantitative methods, and it intends to uncover social processes among workers and managers that can apply to a wider variety of situations.

Anne Tsui and Barbara Gutek (1999) consider that organizational diversity research is qualitative research by definition because it tends to focus on the employment experiences of individuals in minority categories and its preferred methods are case studies. Consequently, a quantitative study along different ascriptive attributes such as gender, age or race can fall under the realm of organizational demography research, because it cannot capture the experiences of working in a diverse workplace. According to Tsui and Gutek (1999), organizational diversity and demography use different methods and purposes.

More specifically, this instrumental case study uses a combination of observational, interview, documentary and survey methods. First, workers were observed on the shop-floor as they did their jobs, and then the first author did in-depth interviews with 87 workers in 16 different teams. These production teams were selected based on their diversity and from both the first and second shifts (see Appendix 2). The second author interviewed workers who previously worked for Kaizen Motors, especially African-American employees. Secondly, the first and second author met and interviewed managers in diversity, human resources and corporate affairs about diversity programs. Third, we analyzed corporate reports about diversity and teamwork. And fourth, we analyzed the data from annual employee opinion surveys. Thus, workers views were taken from employee opinion surveys, and manager views from corporate reports. Interviews were transcribed, coded and analyzed with NVIVO 7, reports were analyzed for their content, and opinion survey descriptive results were examined on the computer (Richards, 2005). In writing the text, we replaced each person's name with a randomly selected name without replacement from a list that we generated.

Teamwork at Kaizen Motors.

We first define team and diversity. *Team* is defined as "a group of people who work together to produce products or deliver services for which they are mutually accountable" (Mohrman et al., 1995). Whereas many people work together cooperatively, teamwork is a type of cooperative work that requires interdependence. The essence of teamwork at Kaizen Motors is job rotation. The ideal size of small teams is five to seven members. Typically four teams of five members form a twenty members group at Kaizen. Perceptions on *team performance/ effectiveness* were measured along four dimensions: problem-solving and suggestions, productivity, quality and safety. The *degree of diversity* is measured by the percentage of women and racial minorities in groups. Similar methods were used for temporary workers and workers over forty years old in terms of diversity, though "age" and "employment status" were not used as sampling criteria (see Appendix 2 for the precise measurement of diversity).

Teamwork is the central theme in the organizational culture at Kaizen Motors, but teams and groups have a special meaning. At Kaizen Motors, the concept of teamwork is used interchangeably with group work since it can be applied to small groups of five as well as to large groups of twenty workers. One of the most surprising findings of the study was that workers did not know their team number but they all knew their call and group numbers. Teamwork at Kaizen has a very general meaning and exists as part of the group. Thus the meaning of teamwork at Kaizen is less connected to intimacy, empowerment and self-management and closer to job rotation.

For example, two teams of ten combine to make one group of twenty workers. Because team members rotate jobs between themselves every two hours they take sequential positions on the line. Actually the structure of work on the assembly line does not give much room to interaction between team members (see Figure 2.1). This means that team worker one or T1 rotates jobs with T2, T2 with T3, T3 with T4, T4 with T5, and T5 with T1. Therefore, team members usually engage in more conversations and chat with members of the team on the other side of the line. The interactions between the members of the team are in most cases reduced to the five minute team meetings organized every two hours. During these breaks, the information exchanges and communication between team members are related to safety and quality concerns. Workers need to know which jobs have problems, how they can be fixed or what the most frequent types of defects are. Because they follow in each other's rotations, they can pass valuable information to each other to prevent injuries and fix problems.

Figure 2.1: Group and team structure at Kaizen Motors

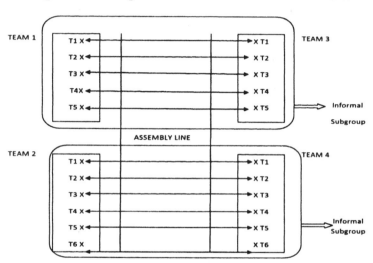

Diversity at Kaizen Motors.

Kaizen Motors strives to move beyond a reactive and defensive approach to make diversity a part of its business strategy. Kaizen Motors's multi-billion dollar diversity investment over the next ten years will be used not only to recruit a diverse workforce and to expand its customer base, also as an organizational strategy to achieve core business objectives and to become an employer of choice. Kaizen Motors clearly has a managed diversity approach, and they seek national recognition as a top diversity organization. They also intend to foster relationships with the entire community and use diversity as a key strategy in global expansion.

Diversity training is an integrated effort at Kaizen Motors. Initially, these diversity courses were offered only to group leaders and upper management, but team members started lately to be involved in diversity awareness sessions. The first two weeks of training of any temporary or full-time member at Kaizen Motors include an anti-harassment video that teaches workers what types of gestures and comments are appropriate or inappropriate. Because it is hard to draw a firm line between an inoffensive or offensive joke, this video sends a very effective message: "Say it only if you would say it also in front of your mother or grandmother!" It is fascinating to follow the connection between teamwork and the family in the creation and enforcement of norms. In some ways, teamwork emerges as a sacred familial space, where love and respect are first and foremost.

Finally, workers are differentiated by their shift assignments. First shift workers included in our sample had the average team tenure of four and a half years and an average organizational tenure of almost twelve years, which showed that they change teams two to three times during their tenure at the plant. Second shift workers in the sample had the average team tenure of a year and a half and the average organizational tenure of six and a half years, which shows that the team turnover is higher in the second shift (workers generally change teams four times during their stay at Kaizen Motors).

Conclusion

As the first sociological work to report on the inside workings of a Japanese transplant, we strive to provide results as insightful as those given by Darius Mehri (2005) and Robert Cole (1974, 1980) on workers in the automotive plants in Japan. Clearly, the diversity found in America and how Kaizen Motors handles it will be entirely different from Japanese plants since there is little diversity there although more women and some immigrants are most recently being hired. This qualitative study will show that many of the processes at Kaizen Motors are intended and straightforward, and some of them are unintended and indirect. But this is often what is uncovered in case studies of organizations, as revealed with the discovery of the informal group going back to the Hawthorne study in the 1930s (Homans, 1950) and as shown in the more recent "radical contradictions" illustrated by Emi Osono, Norihiko Shimizu and Hirotaka Takeuchi (2008) in another Japanese motor company.

Chapter 3

QUEENS OF THE LINE: GENDER AND IDENTITY IN TEAMS

Holy Cow, what have I done? I don't know beans about cars myself, and who's my first team leader, a waitress. What am I going to do? And I thought, I have to teach this girl something. She woops it in there—zip, zip, zip—just like that. She's an extraordinary, outgoing, self-confident individual and she'll do well
Terry Besser Team Toyota

Men take their jobs as a joke, women take it seriously because they know nine times out of ten that they are the ones who bring (the money) home to the children. Most of us are single women, so we have to take our jobs seriously. Men do not. . . .
A woman at Kaizen Motors

It is very empowering for us women to work here. I like doing the same things that men do. I do as good a job as theirs, if not better. I started here out of a fight, because my husband said I cannot do factory work. I wanted to prove him (wrong).
A woman at Kaizen Motors

Working on the line under lean production profoundly affects women team member experiences with physical work, team effort, male co-worker perceptions, and the quality of their family lives. Women go through an identity transformation at Kaizen Motors. Because of their versatility and agility, they can handle the workload as well as men, and in general are excellent employees. They have a sense of satisfaction and pride in their work that is higher than their male co-workers. Sexual harassment is strongly prohibited by Kaizen Motors, so very little overt discrimination has occurred. Men even prefer working with women because they chat and joke to break up the routine of assembly line work, and provide unexpected advice. However, we found two aspects of gender and teams that were not so positive. Kanter's theory about greater numbers of women producing a better environment is not supported because team interactions did not generally improve with more women on each team. And more disquieting, successful teamwork could lead to a host of marital problems in both the men's and the women's families. But each of these factors point to expected and surprising identity transformations that women experienced at Kaizen Motors.

Current findings on how gender influences team performance are mixed. Previous studies on gender in teams reveal no relationship between gender and productivity, with gender having other related negative outcomes in the case of teams performing physically demanding jobs such as feelings of isolation, dissatisfaction, and reduced or lack of attachment (Chattopadhyay, 1999; Riordan and Shore 1997). Other studies raise questions regarding what ratio or percentage of gender diversity that is detrimental to effectiveness. For instance, women did not perceive the highest degree of satisfaction in gender balanced settings or in female settings, but in male-dominated settings (Wharton and Baron, 1991).

Evidence from other studies on auto plants show that women are considered more careful, and consequently, they are charged with the most expensive machinery at Volvo plants (Wallace, 1999). Teamwork can aggravate the nature of the relations between men and women in physically demanding jobs (Rinehart et al., 1997). In Besser's account of the Toyota assembly plant (1996), the maleness of the workforce was initially taken-for-granted (e.g., there were not enough restrooms for women).[1] But this plant does try to support the team building through family-oriented social events for spouses and children (e.g., picnics, Christmas parties, professional baseball games, birthday parties and group pizza lunches).

One female worker reports that "males are trusted more quickly, and were made to feel that they could handle responsibility much sooner." She concludes that there might be sexual harassment at the plant, but it may be better and certainly no worse than many other large manufacturing plants. Besser (1996) follows up on this idea. According to her, the treatment of women in Japanese transplants might not be different from the situation of women in similar US organizations, but the employees have different expectations for a company that emphasizes empowerment, continuous improvement, and teamwork along with family values. Then, the workers feel betrayed and express anger if the company does not live up to these expectations (Besser, 1996).

This project observes how the dynamics of gender and racial relations change when men and women work together for a long time in a similar Japanese plant. The phase of mature lean production undoubtedly leads to a redefinition of gender roles on the lines. This chapter offers a closer look at the contributions and advantages of women in teams, their experiences on the line, women and leadership, sexual harassment and discrimination, as well as at the connection between their work and family (affairs and dating among team members, family time pressures, family conflict, and divorce).

Kaizen Women: Skills, Abilities and Repetitive Work

The question of how women's skills and abilities affect or influence team-work was addressed for each gender: "What is it like to be a woman and to do this kind of work?" and "What are the advantages and disadvantages of working with women on the same team?" Work is redesigned to allow tall or short and slim or heavy workers regardless of their gender to perform to their full capacity. For instance, if you are not very strong, you may ask for tool balancers or hoists to lift heavy parts, or if you are short, you may request for a platform to lift you up. Women may also request lighter guns because they have smaller hands. In one of the heaviest manually lifting parts of assembly, workers have to pull heavy body parts, such as the windshield glass, for instance, which weighs 30 to 35 pounds, but the *takt* time is so fast that some women feel that they do not have the time to use hoists, which takes a toll on their bodies in the long run. When these types of adjustments do not work (workers are too tall or too short), workers are transferred to other teams, so that they can avoid damaging ergonomic positions.

The repetitiveness of this work is physically daunting, and some female workers think that some jobs are not set up with a female in mind. Some women prefer to learn the new jobs from female trainers based on the assumption that females learned to do these jobs in a different, less physical way. For instance, females assemble the body parts of a car in a more gentle and careful manner than men who just slam them in. However, if one best way for women and another best way for men were to be encouraged, standardized work, as the core of lean production, would be compromised throughout the plant.

Male team members no longer question each woman's ability to do this type of work as they did in the initial phase of production. They appreciate that the most important thing that guarantees' someone's success on the line is to come to work with an "I can do anything" type of attitude. Following the "equal, but different" perspective, they observed that whereas men have more upper body strength, women tend to have a lot more lower body strength. Douglas, a male team member, notices:

> This is rough for women. I think about it all the time, but Jackie and Connie beat me up, and I am a guy in pretty good shape. Both of them are petite. Jackie weighs 100 pounds. Connie is 4'11'', has quick little bitty hands and I can put her against any guy here.

Catherine, a team member, confesses:

> It's hard to be a woman and to work here, but it's something that I wanted to do. It's tough. I had sometimes problems with the process, because you need a lot of upper body strength. When I mentioned this to my group leader, he said: "I don't look at you as a woman. I look at you as a team member."

The easiest way to identify a generalized other is when a person refers to "them." The key to finding "multiple generalized others" and "multiple selves" is to locate who might be in the different "they's" being discussed. One male interviewee told us "You guys [i.e., women] are completely different from us." It suddenly struck us that men develop a notion of a "feminine other" since the interviewer was a women. Yet there was little resemblance between my skills and abilities as a sociologist and their skills and abilities as women on the assembly-line. The professed upper-body strength of men and lower body strength of women are also dimensions of "masculine other" and "feminine other." In the end, the team leader tries to simplify the complicate intricacies of selves by minimizing the feminine self and maximizing the team member identity ("I don't look at you as a woman. I look at you as a team member"). Lauren, a team member, shares an equipment modification story:

> Height is an issue for women here. I am 5'4", and there were times when I had to jump in the air to reach the *andon* cord. My team leader saw that I struggle and went immediately to tell that he is afraid for my safety, that I might be injured. They had to make a tool for me to pull the hook down to me so I can build the car.

Both men and women do not consider strength as the most important ability or quality that makes a good worker in the auto factory.[2] A team leader with more than fifteen years of experience in working with different teams and groups noticed that women have quicker hand speed, whereas men have bigger and slower hands. Men therefore are more likely to work in chassis. Agility and versatility is a required quality, therefore petite and slim women may sometimes have an advantage over men if they have to get into small spaces or under cars.

Women and Heavy Work

The first impression that strikes you when you talk to the Kaizen men and women is that they are not tall, heavy built, or particularly muscular. The assembly line has its own natural process of selection. The men and women of the plant who made it over the years are predominantly slim and very fit. Many of them lose an average of 25 pounds during their initial adjustment to assembly line work. But if the worker was overweight when he/she came to Kaizen Motors, he/she may lose as much as 60 to 70 pounds. As Michelle puts it,

> Nobody can walk in here and do it. It is a mental-physical combination, if you are a man or a woman. Some people cannot handle the pressure you are under, the fast pace. It's a mindset. You have to get this frame of mind that this is what you have to do and you will do it.

The teams with the lowest number of women or no women at all are located in chassis, which is where workers install fuel lines, break lines, and fuel tanks. This is the most physically demanding work in the plant. A male team member said that he understands why no women have been assigned on their line in the last four years. Men are also transferred to other lines if they are too short and if they struggle ergonomically with the jobs in chassis. Other men considered the absence of women on chassis line as a form of reverse discrimination. They were told that the line used to have women, but they ended up hurt, and consequently, they were assigned to other stations. It led some of the men think that the company uses double standards of performance for men and women.

Also both men and women can be stronger at certain jobs than others in the normal rotation of jobs. For instance, some workers enjoy installing the front seats, which are heavier, more than putting rubber bands around the doors, which involves more push from the shoulders, wrists, and elbows. Team members frequently mention trade-off arrangements across gender lines in the job rotation cycle. These trade-offs are informally negotiated between the men and women of the team without involving their team leaders or group leaders. Team leaders do not usually care about these arrangements, as long as they do not imply that some workers have to do more work than they should normally do. Here is how Lloyd, a male team leader, expresses his opinion on this kind of trade-off:

> The woman in my team is just as good as any men I've got. There are some jobs she just does not care for, like going underneath the bumper. They are not physical, but she does not like them. She will do jobs that are a lot harder. She just did not get the hang of it. Typically it does not happen to trade off jobs. I wouldn't say that this is a woman's problem. It's just hers. We have men that come in saying that the shoulder is killing them, and that they would like to trade off, too.

However, in the sixteen teams included in this study, it was only the women who asked for trade-offs with the men, and not the other way round. Team members and team leaders seemed to be sensitive to the issues of fairness and equality. Men expect the work to be done if you are a woman or not, because men and women receive equal pay. Male workers said that they try to help a woman the same way they would help a guy. A few men refuse to trade-off jobs and complain that their colleagues tend to "baby sit" women that some men find attractive. This leads to some tension between the men who trade jobs with women and those who do not.

Female and Male Teams

Women function at their best in teams with one or two other women. About half the women said that they prefer to work with men, and that they prefer to be the only female on the team. The other half did not have a preference working with more women or men. Contrary to Kanter's findings on role encapsulation—tightened control and enhanced pressure to perform—half of the women did not seem to suffer because of their token status (being the only woman on a team), while half of them really enjoyed being the "queen of the teams." But why do the Kaizen women enjoy and prefer what appears to be tokenism? First of all, women have enormous pride and satisfaction working in a male domi- nated field, which is associated with power and prestige. The money that Kaizen women earn and the challenging opportunities for professional development have an empowering effect. Secondly, some women do not want competition from other women because they enjoy getting the males attention. Contrary to the situation described by Kanter (1977a, b), women in the low diversity teams exposed what we call the *queen of the team syndrome:* being the only woman in a team is a more privileged than an encapsulated position. As a result, women enjoy the attention associated with token status.

The strength of this interpretation comes from team members' comparisons of working on different mixed, male and female teams while being at Kaizen Motors for ten to fifteen years. Women justify their choice by saying that women get along with men better than with women. Obviously this is not the attitude of all women in all work situations, but at this Kaizen plant, most women believe that men are more relaxed and laid back, and that men are not as easily offended as women. Women also get a lot of respect from men for being able to put up with the work on the line, and Kaizen Motors (especially Human Resources) reinforces this respect as being one of the corporation's fundamental values.

Relationships between women are often described as cattiness, nitpicking and bickering (e.g. "doesn't matter stuff, what somebody is wearing, how her hair is"). This is contrary to the classical stereotype that women are more toler- ant. Women in female teams report that they are also a lot more graphic in their conversations than they would be in the presence of men. Women say that they have the same experience with working with women at other previous work- places, not only at Kaizen Motors.

Some group leaders find that female teams have more relationship prob- lems, and that even the Human Resources Department is aware of this. Nicholas, the only man in a female team, describes a similar experience:

> In a female team, it is a lot more drama. They could not get along, and I got caught up in the middle being the only man. I wouldn't say women are like that, but just these particular women. They would complain about anything. They did not like the rotations, the jobs . . . they would bring their problems from home to work. I just stood back and let it happen, I tried to keep my mouth shut. I wanted to stay out of it. We, the men, get together and laugh about it. You get in trouble if you get involved. They try to involve us too, but I stay strong. I was in that team for five years, so I put up with it for awhile, and then I decided to transfer. I even left day shift for night shift and I enjoyed that. I felt that they went to HR enough, so I did not want to complain about it, too.

Sam went through the same experience and strongly believes that there is "gossiping and cat fighting" between women even in balanced teams (two women and two men). Men feel caught in the middle of the rivalries between the two women. This male team member describes how uncomfortable this situation makes him feel because both women would come to talk to him about the other person and the other way round. Women were pressuring him to take sides, but he remained neutral and befriended both of them.

For the most part, male and female team members were not eager to report their dislikes about other team members. Two men working in female teams reported that they are not "bothered" to work in female teams, and that it does not make any difference after you get used with it. But these male workers exposed more of a resigned attitude than excitement that they work in female teams, which is different from the experiences of females in otherwise male teams, who obviously enjoy their tokenism. Thus, in teams where there was only one man, we were not able to identify a *king of the team syndrome*.

However, we discovered an interesting interaction between gender and age that can improve interpersonal relationships in the long run. The standard high school type of bickering in female teams carries on into the adult years, and then it fades away after people become more mature. Calmness in teams seems to be a product of the longevity of both the team and the team members. After the initial storming stage, women who worked for a long time together start feeling more like sisters than rivals, and men become a bit more like brothers.

This is not to say that male teams are free from competition, rivalry, and arguing. They can be just as bad as female teams. It is sometimes hard to be a man in a team of males because there is a macho attitude of picking on the weaker guys. Richard describes this experience:

> There is more competition between us when there are more males. It's like a basketball game, a lot of competition. What could you win? Just the chance to trash somebody. . . . There is also a lot of trash talking when there are only men. Guys are harder on one another. We joke a little harder. We are pretty harsh about how we do on the job. If somebody is behind, we tease him: What is your problem? Did you have a bad night? A bad weekend? It's the football game? Or "Look at that sissy, he cannot keep up."

However, team members notice that although men may get mad at each other, they do not stay as mad as women. If men get into a fight, two days later they talk to each other, whereas women stay mad for a longer time. They also show different emotions when they are upset: women cry, whereas men tend to curse. But after expressing these emotions, the women and men quickly go about their work.

Men's Views of Women at Work

Women seem to be catalysts of communication and information-sharing in teams. The general perception of team members at Kaizen Motors is that women like to talk and are easier to talk to. They are said to be more forthcoming, open to discussions and to speak their mind. Male team members often seek help and advice from women regarding their personal relationships. Hence, teamwork offers an in-depth understanding of the psychology of the opposite sex, which can be used in marital relationships. Some men say that working side by side with women opened their eyes about what works or does not work in their personal relationships, so it brings more gender awareness. Gregory asks women for advice about improving his relationships because, in his perspective, men have a problem with committing to long-term relationships whereas women seem to be more able to sustain them. Gregory puts it this way:

> I like working with women. I always have. It's not that you mess around (on) your wife, but you gain perspective if she gets upset on you and you do not know why. If I ask my male friend, he tells me: "You know women: they are all crazy." That's the answer you get from a guy. The women will say: "Let's go back and find out what lead to that." You remember you forgot her birthday was last week. They will wake you up.

The blurring division between work and home is evident in this case. The team is gradually moving from a secondary to a primary role as a major agent of gender socialization.

Preference for Working with Women

Joking and chatting are among the most desirable activities to pass time on the line. The work is so repetitious and automatic that having a talkative and bubbly colleague on the other side helps time go by. Men prefer to work with women in their team not because of their physical abilities, but mostly because their chat breaks the boredom of the line. As many of them put it, women spice up discussions, and talk about different topics other than golf and NASCAR races. Some men like to talk more to women than men because their conversations involve gas prices, sales, kids, and "family stuff" rather than rehashing sports. The line brings a new dimension of masculinity into play: men who enjoy talking about family as much as women. Talking is an escape from the tyranny of the line that is treasured by workers regardless of their gender. At the same time, they have to be careful about their language.

Team and group leaders almost unanimously prefer to have more women on their teams, possibly because they have received more diversity training, but also because their long experience with teams gave them the chance to notice the contributions that women bring to teams.[3] Team leaders feel that women bring a cohesive atmosphere to the group, which is important to the culture of Kaizen Motors. The blended gender composition of teams gives them a family atmosphere. One male team member said that he feels more comfortable when there are more women around. The presence of women on the line brings not only a new level of calmness, but also a feeling of security. He even went so far as to say that he does not want to work with a male-dominated team again because this resembles work in a prison. Most men did not go this far, but team leaders were generally quite favorable toward having women on their teams.

Team leaders notice that women talk things through more, are not intimidated about asking questions, and have on average, better communication skills and more creativity. They also seem to be more determined than many of the men on the plant. Women are also more engaged in social activities such as a lunch with a seasonal theme and encouraging healthier eating choices. A team leader observed that it is nice to work after a woman on a job because their areas are usually neat, clean and tidy because they have more finesse and are detail oriented. Another team leader appreciates that women bring calmness to teams while men can be rowdy.

Advantages and Disadvantages of Working with Women in Teams

Of the sixty-six male team members interviewed, 24% said that they prefer to work in teams with more women, 17% preferred to work in teams with more men, and 60% said that they do not have any preference for men or women and that the gender composition of teams does not matter. While 71% of men mentioned no disadvantages in working with women on the same team, 29% of sixty-six men mentioned scattered disadvantages. These disadvantages were: (1) women like to trade-off jobs; (2) women have less physical ability to do overhead work and lifting, which leads men to do more; (3) women are more often on restriction due to injuries, which gives the hardest jobs to men; (4) men have to watch their language around women for fear of being accused of sexual harassment; (5) women on teams leads to flirting and dating; and (6) women cause more gossiping and less cohesion in teams. These percentages are quite small and range from 8% of men for the first three reasons to 3% for the last three.

The first advantage of having more women on teams is that diverse teams provide a better pool of different perspectives, which is especially useful in problem-solving situations. A second advantage is that men feel that women are more detail-oriented, quality conscious, attentive to their surroundings, and are quick learners. As a result, they are more likely to fix defects and take countermeasures. Third, men mention the attention that women give to safety. Many men are carried away by their macho attitudes and are inclined to give an extra effort when it is not appropriate. If women are on their team, they draw attention to ergonomic problems and often prevent injuries from happening. And fourth, women bring a certain compassion and empathy, which builds team cohesion. The gendered contributions of men and women on team performance are important, especially in these areas of problem solving, quality, safety, and productivity.

Problem-solving. The participation rate of women and minorities in the *problem solving* activities that go on in quality circles is considerably higher than the company average, but we have to keep in mind that even the office staff can participate in quality circles. For instance, 34% of women and 31% of minority workers participate in quality circles whereas the overall participation is 21%. The situation is completely different when it comes to participation in suggestion systems. Only 6% of women and 7% of minority workers participate in suggestion systems comparing with 12% participation rate in the company overall (Kaizen Motors corporate records 2006).

The philosophy of *kaizen* or continuous improvement requires workers to meet every two hours to discuss quality, safety and other challenges that team members have on the job. Work on the assembly-line demands increased awareness of problems, and workers sometimes have to find spontaneous or quick solutions to problems. Many of them said that they do not even attempt to use the formal suggestion system anymore because it is very hard to get one accepted. It seems that the *kaizen* system of continuous improvement reached a maturity level at which it is hard to come up with a totally innovative solution. So, when we mention suggestions in this study, we are most often referring to the informal suggestions and solutions that team members look for in daily team activities.

Regarding the impact of gender on daily activities involving suggestions and problem-solving, 37 team members consider that gender is irrelevant when it comes to problem-solving and suggestions, 22 team members consider that men are usually more active, 18 team members consider that the contributions to problem-solving of men and women to be equal, and 10 team members feel that women are more active with suggestions and problem-solving. The general perception is that contributions to suggestions and problem-solving are heavily influenced by the seniority and experience on the job, not by gender. However, some team members consider that men are more active with suggestions because they are more comfortable with industrial settings and are more ambitious about their jobs. Women are usually vocal about suggesting improvements and solutions because their bodies break down more, so they are directly interested in making their jobs easier.

However, gender has something to say about how a suggestion is received by the team. Women make more suggestions, but not necessarily better suggestions, and men seem to be more successful in getting their points across. Consequently, some women transfer their suggestions to men for presentation to the team, and the men also often get the implementation and evaluation duties. A male team member explains that a woman, especially if she is the only woman on the team, will shy away from bringing her suggestion forward during team meetings, and will often ask men to present her idea to the group: "Hey, Mark, why don't you tell them about this?"

Quality. As a second dimension of team performance, the problem solving skills of women are closely related to contributions to *quality*. When the workforce at Kaizen was surveyed about quality, there are some interesting gender differences: (1) 55% of team members responded that gender does not influence quality, (2) 20% of team members believe that men and women are equally concerned with quality, (3) 18% find women to be more quality conscious, and (4) 7% see men as more quality conscious. Although 75% of team members say that gender is not an important aspect of quality, three times as many workers (18% compared to 7%) find women more quality conscious than men. This aspect of quality is tricky because, as one team member puts it, "men might manage to do the work in time but their quality is not right, whereas some women might struggle with the job because they want to turn in a perfect quality product."

Two reasons were given for women contributing more to quality: (1) women are more quality conscious and detail-oriented, and (2) women are more conscientious about their work, aware of their environment, and likely to catch defects. Some team members feel that men are more task-oriented and concerned about getting their work done quickly, while women are more detail-oriented and concerned with the quality and appearance of the product. A few men said that women are perfectionists, and that they want everything to be neat and clean (e.g. "it wrecks their brains if they have a defect").

Logan, another male team member, attempts to explain why females on his team have an "obsession with quality" by comparing men and women athletes in the Olympics: "They never cross the boundaries like the male athletes. They have more finesse. It's the same here." Family is often brought into the discussion as an explanation for women's preoccupation with quality. Women's interest with detail and appearance comes from the fact that they take care of the house and their children, where everything has to be neat and well organized. Again, there is a spill-over effect of family and team.

However, even though women are considered more quality-conscious, team members insist that this does not mean that women's overall quality is better than men's. For instance, as women tend to talk more than men on the job, this could prove detrimental to their focus causing more defects than men. Also, they might not be very careful with quality if they cannot keep up with the pace of the job. Nick gives us an example of how a predominantly male team responded to the pressures of a quality-conscious lady:

> She was born with it. It is her nature to pay attention to all the details. We are happy when she pats us on the shoulder about a defect. She grabs the team leader: "Hey, look this guy missed something down the line!" We are not upset, no way! It saves us thirty minutes, because the whole group has to be here after shift to fix the problem. So we tell her: "Thank you! We go home early thanks to you."

Safety. The third contribution of safety is a number one priority at Kaizen Motors. As a result, it is not surprising that over 50% of workers (50 of 87) consider that safety should be promoted by everybody regardless of gender. Only one man felt that men were more safety conscious than women, while 17 team members said that women were more safety-conscious and 19 team members found both genders to be equally safety-conscious. One reason why women are more safety conscious is that women are not as strong and have to protect their bodies more. Administrative records show that women have a higher percentage of cumulative injuries (38.2% instead of the average of 21%) but fewer acute injuries (12.8% instead of 21%). These records are consistent with our qualitative data that show that women have safer work habits. Women explain men's higher incident rate by their macho attitude that they cannot get hurt. Janice states that: "Guys feel they are tough and can't and won't get hurt. They are risk-takers and their egos get them in trouble." Men agree that some of them want to get the work done without taking care of safety, and many are more reckless with their bodies than women. John remarks that when a piece of machinery is broken, men on their team will continue to work, but the woman will stop and wait until that piece is fixed.[4]

Productivity. And finally, in the fourth area of contributions, team members unanimously agreed that men and women have equal *productivity* on the line. Much of this is due to being on an assembly line that is paced the same *takt* time for everyone. Men and women who cannot keep up with the pace of the line eliminate themselves or can be fired regardless of gender. Consequently, productivity did not seem to be an issue to most men and women—"if you don't keep up, you're gone."

Gendered Interactions in Teams

One might think that after team members work with each other for ten or more years that gender would not matter anymore, but this is not the case. Despite the company's rhetoric of assimilating women into teams, sensual talk and humor are still present in the daily interactions of teams. Patricia, a 38-year old single mother had just returned from two weeks medical leave for breast augmentation surgery. Although already quite attractive, she was very happy with her recent operation and also quite open about it with her male colleagues. She explains that she is proud of them for being so nice and supportive. Evan, one of her male colleagues, however, agrees that they are very close to each other in the team but reveals that when: "Patricia had the boob job, everybody knew it about it . . . she got some ribbing about it." The other men gave her a hard time.

A moving story of helping behavior in diverse teams involves Laura, a 53-year old female worker. She recently had to cope with the death of her husband, and soon after that she was diagnosed with breast cancer. Laura came back to work six weeks after the surgery, and started to adjust slowly to assembly-line work like the rest of the workers who come back from restriction (a week of one hour on and one hour off). She did not try to look for other easier jobs because she wanted to make as much money as she can, so she can be a greeter at Wal-Mart after she retires. Terence, the team leader, explains how the whole dynamic of the team changed upon receiving the news that Laura had cancer:

> It was devastating to learn she has cancer. They were all grieving. They all encompass her. She came back after double vasectomy and nobody could hold her down. She is a strong woman. We kind of buffered her a little bit. She did not want to be slow on medical. It was also the monetary issue of being out. We compromised and gave her a good rotation, and the whole team supported that. It was not a question. She is strong now as she's ever been. She is stronger now because she realizes how much everybody cares about her.

A team leader tells a story of grieving and mourning connected to one of his men who died in a car crash. All the team members pulled together as a team, carpooled, and went to his funeral. What is fascinating about these stories is the *in vivo* concept of grieving in teams. Grieving is a sign of the close relationships that can develop between team members over the years, and it is the ultimate symbol of the team as a family or community of fate. We grieve or mourn only close family members or friends, not mere acquaintances or strangers.

Talk and chat are central aspects of male and female interactions in teams. The major discomfort perceived by men in mixed teams is related to the fact that they have to constantly practice censorship in their conversations. For example, one male worker says: "we have to watch our language...we are not allowed to be rude or lewd." In other words, the most significant discomfort in mixed teams does not come from differences in performance, skills, abilities, conflicts or helping behavior, but from elements of team culture. Chatting on the line also involves a lot of teasing, silly talk, and cutting up. After working together for a long time, some teams develop a certain intimacy, and women are treated like some of the guys. Then the men do not feel that they have to hold their guard around the women. After they start being comfortable with each other, nobody likes running to Human Resources to report inappropriate jokes. Women, however, do not feel that they have to watch their language around men, but they notice that male conversations change in the presence of women. Dana indicates that "If they are all in the room, they will not say certain things in front of me just out of respect for me." But teams do vary. Gina decided to match the men "tit for tat" concerning their jokes, and she was then told by her supervisor to be more lady-like. Nonetheless, on the whole diverse team members are an asset for mixed teams because they offer the promise of more exciting and more diversified conversations on the line.

Being a Woman and Working on the Line at Kaizen

For most women, work at Kaizen Motors comes as a culture shock. Some say that work is very hard and strenuous, and if they did not need the money, they would have quit in the first six months. However, the Kaizen Motors Annual Opinion Survey shows that women have a slightly more positive opinion than men about their work at Kaizen Motors. Women are happier and appreciate their jobs more than their male counterparts. What makes women happy here despite the nature of the work and despite the fact that they are a minority on the line? The following series of interviews gives us a glimpse into the reasons why women's experiences are so gratifying. Gina, a team member explains:

> It is very empowering for us, women, to work here. I like doing the same things that men do. I do as good a job as theirs, if not better. I started here out of fight, because my husband said I cannot do factory work. I wanted to prove him. He is shocked that I made it for this long.

Emily, a temp soon to be hired full-time, says: "I will be the breadwinner soon. I will make double than my husband, so he should be at home babysitting."

Full-time workers with little experience can earn up to $50,000 a year including overtime, while more experienced workers bring home $70,000 to $80,000. This is a rare job opportunity for workers who often only have a high-school education. When women with a high school degree having earned $15,000 to $20,000 a year in dead-end jobs manage to double or triple their income, this opportunity liberates them. Thus, it is not surprising that their jobs at Kaizen Motors open them up to a new "generalized other" and self concept. They talk about the cultural shock of working in a male-dominated environment for the first time in their lives. To their surprise, their male colleagues are not making fun of them, but on the contrary, some of them are the "most awesome, respectful and best friends they ever had in their lives. Sheena clarifies in her story:

> I've been very happy so far. You can't find a better job anywhere in this state, unless you have a good education. Most women here are single mothers. We are more dedicated and appreciate somewhat more our jobs here. Money is not so important, but benefits made a big difference. Very good insurance... I have this security. It is so much better than before.

Pamela was in a similar situation:

> I am divorced and have no children. I did not get to finish college, and for me as a woman, it's a good job. I could never make that kind of money elsewhere. I did a lot of secretarial work before and I wasn't happy. I can tell you that you can work as physical but not make this kind of money somewhere else. I worked two full-time minimum wage jobs and did not bring home what I brought home as a temp here. Where I am from [a rural area], men are used to bring home the money. There are not a lot of opportunities for women as there are for men. Men in my family used to make this kind of money, not the women. Women in my family, teachers or nurses, do not make half I make. The stress of not having the money to make it when I had the two jobs, the stress was so mentally affecting and demanding physically . . . was so worried!

Cynthia, a young female worker, shares the same perspective:

> I think women are happier here. My opinion: I am happier to work here than my husband is. I like it better, he hates it. For me, I feel that I did not have to do this kind of job. I chose to do it. Last year he made $70,000 a year, and I made $50,000 a year. I was making $22,000 a year before coming here, so it's double pay. I hear a lot of people complaining about the company. You know what? I tell them: "You should work for a company that does not provide anything and pays you $10 an hour."

Jane, a 45-year old female worker who has been recently hired full-time, describes her journey from factory to factory till she ended up at Kaizen. She asserts that she is so happy with her new job that she regrets that she came here so late in her career:

I can't believe that I got this good job so late in life. The money we get here is a lot better than college-educated people in professional jobs. I am sorry that will be able to work here only 10, maybe 12 more years.

Being a Kaizen worker gives these women more prestige and pride about themselves. The women who come from underprivileged backgrounds are more respected and have a higher status in their families and communities:

People back home think that I am rich. They say: "Oh, my God, you work at Kaizen!" I am glad that I work for a company that I know 25 years from now I can retire from.

Although women are underrepresented in this plant and in this traditional masculine occupation, the dominant emotions that they report in the interviews are those of pride, satisfaction, self-esteem, empowerment, enthusiasm, gratitude etc. Instead of being ridiculed in degradation ceremonies, female workers enjoy an elevated status at Kaizen Motors, which make them feel like the "queens of the teams." This last example shows that shame, embarrassment and stigma are not part of these social interactions. Crying and embarrassment are rather collateral emotions that emerge in the process of social interaction between men and women, while the main ingredients that govern their work are competence, sociability, feeling comfortable, and having fun together. Thus, the data support our initial hypothesis that symbolic interactionist theories capture the positive emotions and the importance of team generalized others in these gendered interactions (Janoski, Grey and Lepadatu, 2007, 2010b).

Women's wealth and new image can attract the unwanted attention of opportunist males. They deal with it in an uncompromising fashion, which is a symbol again of their empowerment. Ashley comments:

I am single now and dating, and as soon as men hear that I work at Kaizen, they say: "Oh, wow, I can quit my job now." You can be sure that I will never go out with that man again. I know they might be joking, but I don't think this is funny.

For the most part, women feel that they have a lot more patience with repetitive work than men. The company statistics show that women have safer behavior at work. The demographic composition of the plant is 21% women and 79% men; however, the percentage of injuries is 18.6% for women and 76.3% for men, whereas the cumulative illness rate is 36% for women and 56% for men. Men and women also report having different types of injuries depending on their height: back problems for men and shoulder problems for women (however, these are only workers' perceptions and not company records). Generally, men think that women are physically and psychologically different from them, but women are not necessarily weaker despite being smaller.

Tina says that she enjoys the work on the line more than behind the desk in a bank. She likes being active and engaged in all sorts of activities, like problem-solving and quality circles. Nevertheless, she is worried because she has no idea how long she will be able to work in assembly.

> I don't even have to think about what I am doing. When they take a part away after a model change, you are still reaching for that part for a week or two. Some people are bored to tears. This job is not for everybody. It takes a personality to do this kind of work. My husband cannot do this kind of work for instance. With the *takt* time, you are really pushing yourself. I hope I can retire from here.

Carey, a 45-year old woman, suffers from carpal tunnel syndrome from installing parts while continuous leaning over car bodies. This is how she describes her impairment:

> My hands will not last me more than eight-nine years if I keep doing this. I sleep at night with wrist braces on because my hands will fall asleep. Wrist braces hold your hands in a certain way so you are not bending them. My hands will fall asleep when I am drying my hair in the morning or when I drive the car for more than an hour.

Elizabeth, an older woman in her mid-fifties, talks about her recovery when she came back from restriction. The recovery of older workers takes more time as opposed to younger workers. She stayed at home five months after her shoulder surgery. When she came back from restriction, she had two weeks of introduction, and during those two weeks, she was allowed to work one hour on and one off, then two hours on and two hours off. Somebody from the second shift was filling in when she was off. Then the team leader told her that she should get on the line because that person has to go back to the second shift. She was basically thrown into the job although she could feel that her body had not healed properly. She had to go back to the assembly line; otherwise, her team members would have to pick up her slack. She says she was rushed into the job and was hurting. She could barely keep up with the *takt* time and could not take the time to check for quality. Jim, a 29-year old male man, thinks that:

> Women are smaller frame on average. These jobs tend to hurt them more. On our line at least, women tend to get hurt more. You can hear sometimes comments like "I wish we will get here people that do not break that much."

At the same time, women are more vocal when they cannot perform a job properly and are more concerned of changes that might affect their health. So, the whole group is pushed to figure out how to make those jobs easier. As a result, the whole group, including men, benefits from the new improvements (i.e., *kaizen*). William, an older team leader with a lot of experience on different teams, explains:

> Women have more cumulative injuries because they are apt to take more pain

than men. I saw my wife giving birth. I couldn't do that. Women deal with pain. They rather work with it. That's my personal opinion. As soon as a man hurts, he will let somebody know because he does not want to let his family down, if he is the breadwinner.

That women are able to take more pain is only part of the explanation. The high rate of cumulative injuries is also explained by the fact that women start the "second shift" as soon as they arrive at home. They only relax their hands during sleep because they have to take care of most of the household duties using their hands (Hochschild, 1990).

Female Team Leaders

Three out of eleven team leaders from the sample were women. Female team leaders seemed to be very comfortable in their authority position of leading men in a male-dominated environment. Briona, a female team leader for three years, confirms that her authority was rarely challenged:

I had issues only a couple of times with a couple of men who came in the team thinking that they do not have to listen to me because I am a woman. I told them that unfortunately I am the boss and we all have to keep our jobs. Being an African-American leader was never an issue for me. When a female team leader tells a man that he did not do something right, it bothers him only if he is insecure, if he does not know who he is.

As this interview shows, Briona mentions her multiple selves (e.g. being an African-American and female leader).[5] This statement implies that her team members develop different concepts of the generalized other that sometimes clash with each other. Since team leaders' main responsibilities are teaching, training, scheduling, quality and safety, they are not in the traditional supervision position of exerting control and power over subordinates. Meagan, another female team leader, offers her perspective:

Some men might not appreciate having a woman team leader. I do not set rules really, I enforce rules. I do more teaching and training. I enjoy it because I do so many different things. I am not interested in moving up to the position of group leader, because I have a daughter to take care of.

Although they are more comfortable with female leaders when they ask for time to go to the restroom, female team members do not necessarily prefer to work with female instead of male team leaders. Break times are scheduled every two hours, but five minute breaks are sometimes too short to go the bathroom or the bathroom might be too crowded. So team members can press the *andon* cord when they are on the line and ask for emergency relief. Two female workers said that they would prefer to have female team leaders because they could tell them about their struggles with the job from the very beginning.

Sexual Harassment and Discrimination

The general attitude of the Kaizen women was that they do not want to receive any kind of special treatment or favoritism from the company. Angela is adamant about this issue:

> They should not make different regulations for women because it is reverse discrimination. They should not change their business for us. I took this decision to come and work here in the factory. If I cannot do the job at the same level as a man, I should not be here.

However, some male workers accuse some of their colleagues of helping the more attractive women on their teams, and blame leaders for being more sensitive to women's issues. When asked how men and women get along in her team, Gina agrees that:

> There is favoritism, a certain in-company politics that you have to play. A pretty smile on your face can take you pretty far. I don't know why guys complain about it. For guys, if you play golf or hang out at Applebee's, you will go a lot further than the ones who don't. We also have to play the old boys game. If you want to be on a certain circle, and if you have an interest in advancing, you have to play their game.

The overwhelming majority of women claimed that Kaizen Motors is the best employer they ever had, that they do not feel discriminated against because of their gender, and that their male colleagues are the most respectful and nice colleagues they ever worked with. The firing process in the Japanese system is usually very lengthy. It is peer review based and usually gives the worker three chances to improve. However, sexual harassment is the quickest way of being fired at Kaizen Motors.[6]

There were only a small number of women who reported sexual discrimination or sexual harassment incidents in teams. Many of these reports were not of the level that would generate an investigation. For instance, Joyce, a female team member, clarifies this apparent grey area:

> It is a little discrimination. If a guy says something, it is accepted immediately, but if we say something like women, we have to prove it is right. We are yelled at more easily than at men. They are afraid that we will break some machinery. It is assumed that a man knows what he is doing, and he will not break anything, but they forget that some of us have been doing this for such a long time.

Jocelyn explains:

> We do not get any special treatment. I like this equality that Kaizen promotes here. I know a team leader who harassed a temporary twice. He invited her to his vehicle outside, and his wife worked here too. If you speak to me like that, I

will let you know upfront how I feel. He is my neighbor and I was in (shock) . . . when I heard this.

Diane follows on the same line:

> Here they make a point of diversity. Anti-harassment is driven in your head. Now even the male chauvinists pigs keep their opinions to themselves. At other places I worked in you are discounted if you are a woman. Most people are helpful here. Some are idiots, but they will always be. They will dismiss you, talk down to you, make things hard on you, trying to go fast and slam you, this kind of thing. . . .

Other reports of sexual harassment were more serious. Team members reported three cases when female temps were reassigned to their teams as a follow-up to sexual harassment allegations. These women appeared to be poorly integrated into their new teams particularly because of their lack of trust with men. Although these adoptive groups tried to include them and communicate with them during breaks and lunches, these women avoided interactions with their new team members. One of them even said: "If this is not related to work, I do not have to answer you." Finally, team members complained about their limited integration and consequently, the women were reassigned to female teams, where they probably felt more comfortable and secure. Their behavior is evidence that they probably have post-harassment traumatic symptoms that make it hard for them to reestablish trust and reintegrate into mixed teams. Gwendolyn remembers her experience as a female temp having to deal with a team leader "who did not like women":

> When I was a temp, I went home and cried at one time. I resented him, because he was rude. He said to me one day: "We need you on line 1", and then he said he hates to send me over there because that team will have overtime. By the end of the day, he told them: "You can keep her. She is useless anyway." I tried to look like I was OK, but I went home and cried. . . . I was devastated. It did bother me because we were right on time, and I worked as hard as anybody here. My problem is that I do not act like being into them [team leaders]. It would have been an easier way if I flirted with him, showing to him that he is the man. . . .

George, a black male group leader, describes how he solved a heated argument between a male and female team member in his group. He said that "as a group leader, [he] make[s] sure [he] look[s] everybody in the eye" and that he is "not interested in anything below your neck." The incident could have easily degenerated into a case of sexual harassment:

> I have to enforce dressing codes, make sure they do not have tops too loose, too revealing. Sometimes they might need a definition. One male team member made a negative comment about his colleague's outfit . . . that she is exposing too much. She was in tears because somebody judged her on anything other than her work ethic, and it hurt her. . . . I understood her because I also have

daughters. I asked myself: "If this is my daughter, what would I do?" So, I walked up to my locker and gave her one of my extra T-shirts. I did not say anything to her and just left the room, walked away.

Group and team leaders, like George, are constantly under the pressure of just-in-time production, and must know how to properly manage the challenges of working with a diverse workforce.

Each year, full-time team members at Kaizen Motors have to watch an anti-harassment video that is showed in the cafeteria during the lunch break. It is also mandatory for all the temporary workers to watch this video before they sign their contracts with the temporary staff agencies. Sexual harassment is defined as uninvited and unwelcome verbal or physical behavior of a sexual nature especially by a person in authority towards a subordinate, but sexual harassment lawsuits are surrounded by controversy because sometimes the lines between appropriate and inappropriate behavior at work can be blurry. Therefore, Kaizen Motors conveys a very clear message in these anti-harassment videos: "Do not say anything to your colleague which you wouldn't say to your mother or grandmother!" The message basically encourages team members to have very close interpersonal relationships with each another, but they should not venture into risky territory.

Redefining Femininity and Masculinity on the Line

Are these team members superwomen? One male worker says that "it has to take a special woman to incorporate herself in this male environment." Although both female and male workers agree that strength is only one aspect of successful performance on the line, it was surprising that a female worker praises the good work of another female colleague with the label "you are a he-woman." She obviously internalizes the norms and gender roles of a society that associates masculinity with power and strength. Other women demystify their aura of being special women: "If I can do it, anybody can do it. You just have to be patient. This is not for superwomen."

One might expect women working at a traditional masculine job to exhibit early aging or masculine habits, but these women do not have male characteristics, attitudes or gestures. They are far removed from showing off their muscles as Rosie the Riveter did in the World War II poster, and are closer to the fragility of Norma Rae (played by Sally Field in the movie with the same title). The tough screening process that workers have to go through before they are hired allows managers the chance to observe the pool of applicants on numerous occasions. Hiring at the Kaizen Motors plant is a very selective process (a worker said that when he was hired, he was a member of a twenty-worker cohort selected from a pool of more than 4,000 applicants). So, if we take into consideration that these workers are the cream of the crop, then it is safe to say that these women and men are special workers. They are very professional, intelligent, and well-spoken, and they exude dynamism, enthusiasm and femininity. They are smaller frame, petite and slim women, who are very careful about their physical appearance. They wear nice and sometimes sexy T-shirts and camisoles and sometimes big earrings, although they were told earrings are safety hazards. Many of them put make-up on every single day at work and have highly polished nails. Few of them feel that it is necessary to pull their hair back, and many wear fashionable haircuts instead. It is difficult to keep their long nails clean and intact, and some of them say that they cannot even work without the nails, because it protects the top of their fingers. And they never break a nail! All this indicates that they do not neglect their interpretation of feminine identity and this is possibly a sign that they enjoy the attention and status of being among the few women in the plant. Carey confesses:

> I want to be a woman, a pretty tough one, and they [men] let me be one too. I don't have to act like a man. I always wear make-up. It is my ritual, my vanity issue. I get a lot of attention, but I just smile and say: "Thanks."

Gladys, an attractive 38 year-old woman with well coiffed hair, is the only woman who admits that it is hard for her to preserve her femininity on the line. She explains that she did not want to do this for the rest of her life because it is hard to be "womannie-womannie" and "girly here."

The visible display of femininity seems to be an important element of life in predominantly male settings. Women recruits in the Marine Corps are required to wear make-up, long hair arranged in an "attractive, feminine way" and skirted uniforms. They are also discouraged from acting macho, but urged to act more like "ladies," so they are encouraged to expose their femininity in a more appealing way. Christine Williams (1992) explains that this type of femininity display in male-dominated occupations reflects men's insecurity about their own gender identity. Williams' study about the early inclusion of women in the Marine Corps shows that when men see women accomplishing tasks that they regard as masculine, their own masculinity is threatened. However, this military situation is different from Kaizen Motors, mostly because men and women spent almost twenty years working side by side in this non-traditional field.[7]

Conclusion

This chapter on women illustrates four major findings. First, women go through an identity transformation at Kaizen Motors. Because of their versatility and agility, they can handle the workload as well as men, and in general are excellent employees. Their group identity as expressed through the generalized other changes from a defensive group of women to a multi-gendered and diverse team. Their individual identities as women include a sense of satisfaction and pride in their work that is greater than that of their male co-workers. Women at Kaizen Motors feel empowered because of their high wages, the self-esteem that they receive resulting from doing well in a "man's world," and the respect and attention that they receive from their male co-workers. As a result, their individual identities are strongly female, but their group identity favors their teams, which constitute and consume so much of their lives.

Second, men prefer to work with women on teams, but they cite both advantages and disadvantages. The main advantages are the chat and humor between men and women that alleviate the routine and boredom of assembly line work, as well as the family atmosphere that they bring in teams. The disadvantages are the trade-off of jobs, women's perceived physical difficulties in doing overhead work, women's cumulative injuries that put them on restriction more than men, and the fact that men have to watch their language around women.

Third, in the broader picture of diversity, two theories help explain these results. First, the team intensification theory works well for the very reason that it fell out of favor in the general race relations literature. Lean production teams put differently perceived people together with equal status, interlink them in tasks with strong institutional legitimacy, while at the same time achieving a successful outcome recognized by all. With strong management support, team work in lean production fits the contact hypothesis perfectly. As a result, men and women most often stress their team identities and generalized others over gendered others within the plant. At the same time, women's self confidence and individual identities are clearly strengthened. Second, Ely and Thomas' integration and learning theory shows what goes on within the teams. Women contribute a new and stronger view of quality that fits in with the overall goals of quality, and they also added a perception of interest and understanding that made boring work more interesting.

In the opposite direction, Kanter's theory about greater numbers of women producing a better environment is not supported. Team chemistry does not seem to improve with more women on each team. Teams with all men exhibited more rivalry and competition, while teams with all women had had more interpersonal conflicts. Teams with low gender diversity (with only one to two women) had the highest satisfaction because women enjoyed the respect and attention associated with their "queen of the team" status. Whereas the previous studies on Toyota (Besser, 1996; Mehri, 2005), Subaru-Isuzu (Graham, 1995) and Mitsubishi (*New York Times*, 2001) exposed discrimination against women in Japanese factories, this study presents a more optimistic and nuanced picture.

The queen metaphor is a symbol for women's empowerment and higher satisfaction on the job, as well as a symbol of the systematic effort of Kaizen and its suppliers to integrate women in the core functions of production in the US. Despite issues of fatigue, time deprivation, and the high incidence of divorce (to be covered in the next chapter), the queens of the line are clearly the new and resilient winners in the mature phase of lean production.

Chapter 4

SEXUAL ATTRACTION ON THE LINE: FAMILY, AFFAIRS AND TEAM INTENSIFICATION

Darius Mehri's study about work relations in an auto supplier plant revealed that Japanese companies still do not have restrictions on co-workers dating. Supervisors may still play matchmaker, and companies continue the practice of *gōkon*, which is an informal drinking party arranged at a restaurant for employees (2005:57-60). Dating at work is supposed to strengthen the community of fate, a basic feature of Japanese organizations (Besser, 1996). Dating is also a major recurring theme that emerges from the discussions on intra-team relationships between men and women at Kaizen Motors in the US. Grace talks about dating as a general, acknowledged, and undisputable reality in the plant: "You know what they say around about Kaizen. . . . The rumors that go around are about family disruptions." In reinforcing the team intensification theory used here, she explains: "It is because we spend so much time here." The company has a formal policy on relationships stipulating that married couples cannot work together in the same team. In most of the cases, the husband or the wife is assigned to other departments or stations.

Most of the workers that start working at Kaizen Motors lose between twenty to thirty-five pounds in their first six months on the line, and some overweight people loose even fifty pounds. Women in these teams get an immense satisfaction from their weight loss and use their job as a work-out plan. This boosts their confidence and makes them feel more comfortable with their personas.[1] In the long run, these drastic changes of persona might latently contribute to shifts in their personal relationships and divorces down the road. One of the most important reasons that some workers feel "at home" at work is that they are more appreciated, feel more competent at work than at home, and receive emotional support from their colleagues (Hochschild, 1997). Sherry adds another reason:

> I am happy because I lost that many pounds. It makes you feel more attractive. Men treat you better. It is probably more in my head than anything else.

Dating at Kaizen

Although both male and female team members agree that dating at work is counterproductive, they think that it is unavoidable. Janine, a female team member, emphasizes the intensity of teams:

> I spend more time here than with my family. If you think about it, it is so natural that you are going to have some attractions. You are looking at the same Joe every year, he is starting to look hot to you, but people should handle it responsibly!

Elizabeth, another female worker, explains:

> Dating is going to happen here more often than in any other workplace. We are here since early in the morning till late in the afternoon, and when we go home there's so much to do just to catch up. If I was single, I wouldn't have the energy to attempt to go out and date. There is always going to be a little dating when men and women work together. Nobody said anything to me that's been crazy like: "Man, did I just hear that?" I have a good sense of humor. There is always a playful interaction, and you have to laugh along with it. Some people like to run to HR and report everything. There is a difference between harassment and just fun.

The concept of "playful interaction" describes that there should be a chemistry between the men and women of the team. Other team members appreciate that it is more fun when you have women in the group because there is more "innocent flirting" and "silly stuff." For most of the assembly-line workers, these playful interactions and innocent flirting must be ways to escape a tiresome and dangerous job. Janice, a forty year-old single mother, tells about her experience at Kaizen Motors:

> Lord, it helps being attractive. People are trying to get a date with you, it happens all the time. If somebody is married and disrespectful and making obvious advances, you have to cool it down. You ask how is the family, how is the wife, you let them know where you stand. . . . I am a happy single and I do not mess with married men.

Gina, a female team leader, follows up with the same idea:

> Affairs . . . that goes on quite a bit here. Management does not encourage it, but looks the other way. They need to do a study on what the divorce rate is here. I would like to see that. All the women on my team are divorced or single moth-

ers.

It is very interesting that workers predominantly used the word "affair" and not "romance," implying that most of the love affairs that happen at work are between married workers. A male team member, troubled by the high divorce rate, estimates that there are a lot more divorces than marriages in his group and that in the ten years he spent working in his team, eight out of ten colleagues divorced. David elaborates on the topic:

This is a crazy place, men do trade-offs with women for heart issues. This is high-school magnified a hundred percent. There is a lot of dating, jealousy, people switching wives sometimes. People do it all the time. I wouldn't marry somebody here. My wife works first shift, and we see each other over the weekend. Divorce rate is so bad because people do not try enough to save their marriages.

Flirting and dating can cause disruptions and tensions for teams at work. Many workers agree that most of the romances or affairs in teams do not work out in the long-term, and that this leads to many uncomfortable situations. Some such situations involve emotional competitions between workers, and other situations concern working side-by-side with an "ex." Justine, an attractive woman in her mid 40s, describes her experience when she first joined a female team:

This is like back in high school. All of us were young, in our mid 20s and early 30s. It got to a point when I really did not want to come in here. This is how bad it was. When I started seeing this guy, I don't know if it was jealousy, but the other girls stopped talking to me. They like attention, people to stop by. Some of the younger ladies here...they feed on it. When an attractive girl or semi-attractive girl would come to the group, they did not want anything to do with her. Nobody will talk to her. It took them a month till somebody talked to me. It was bad, it was unreal.

But with relationships that start out well, there can be problems that surface over time. In the example of George the team leader who gave the woman a t-shirt in chapter 3, there was more to the story. George goes on to describe the comments made by her ex-boyfriend:

Actually she was going through an ugly break-up and her boyfriend said: "What are you trying to do? Are you putting everything out there?" [i.e., wearing provocative clothing.] It was 99 degrees that day and she just dressed comfortably for a hot day at work.

All being fair in love and war does not always mix well with work on the shop floor, and this is often an overlooked part of diversity policies because it is not easily resolved. Transferring one or the other team member is the rule for marriages, but it is more difficult to insist on transfers with sometimes ephemeral and/or informal dating relationships.

Families Coping with Work at Kaizen

Hochschild (1997) points out how shift work can lead to broken marriages, and assembly lines having their own "marriage busters"—women or men who seduce their co-workers as a source of entertainment. Men sometimes recognize the dangers of dating at work, even while finding it to be a common event on the line. Jack advises:

> I wouldn't marry somebody here, because I am a very protective person, and men are pigs. They hit on any woman walks through. There's a guy on my group that knows every single woman on this plant. It's an assembly thing. Guys turn into dogs even though they are fifty. It's not as bad as it used to be because they can get fired now.

William, a group leader, mentions that his biggest concern on the job is the flirting and dating, which he calls "interpersonal intermingling." As a group leader, he feels that it is very important not to show favoritism to attractive women because in this line of work, team members might touch each other by mistake when they assemble cars.

Work on the line can be detrimental particularly to couples who work on opposite shifts. Some of the workers said that there are days when they do not get to see their spouses at all, but they try to compensate by calling each other during the breaks. The night shift seems to have its own different pace, rules and culture:

> We are living in a totally different time zone. The world is a lot smaller on the night shift. If you have a first-shift person at home, and you work in a different time zone, the companionship is not there. You only meet over the weekend, and we have to work Saturdays now. You have to work harder to make your relationship work and nowadays people don't do this.

Only one female worker advises that working in an opposite shift with her husband helps their family because there is always an adult at home to take care of their four children. This is particularly important for taking care of sick children. Although you would expect that the divorce rate is higher in the second shift than in the first shift, we should keep in mind that night shift workers are very young and still in the early stages of their relationships. It is more likely for first shift workers to be at their second and possibly third marriage. Kathleen, a female worker, describes the story of her divorce:

> My ex-husband worked here, and I thought it was a good opportunity for me, too. We had problems in the past, and it intensified here. He was very jealous. Any break or lunch he had to be with me. I felt like I wasn't trusted. You put a lot of people together, and this is what happens. People say things to you all the time, but they do not say tacky things. People say that I am attractive. People

top and talk to me all the time. I can't stop it. I wouldn't date somebody here again because people are jealous. The divorce rate here is very bad.

But for other women, having this kind of job helps them leave bad or abusive relationships. Kimberley tells us:

I was married for ten years, and wanted to be in a position to take care of me and my kids to get out of a really bad marriage relationship. Kaizen gave me the means to take care of my family. I divorced soon after I came here.

At the same time, assembly-line romances work well for others. Especially for the young workers in the night shift, marrying somebody from the same group works great because it is hard to date somebody from outside the plant at those "weird" hours, as they call them. Couples are protected from breaking up if they are not poisoned by the jealousy factor, especially since this is a working environment where men and women might work closely side by side, shoulder to shoulder, and might even touch each other unintentionally during the production process. When the marriage works out, people can see clearly the advantages of marrying one of their co-workers. Work at such an intensified pace is very demanding on workers' bodies and minds. If they marry a co-worker, they not only get a well paid spouse, but they also get a supporter who completely understands the hard work they have to put up with everyday. Jacyln, a female worker, realizes that:

It helps to have my husband here. I never understood the aches and pains. Now I see it and feel it by myself. I know how it is to work here and how you interact with people all day long. I can understand that he has to talk to other women, and I understand as long as I do not see him doing it.

However, if both husband and wife do assembly-line work, then both will be beat up when they get home. Being physically and mentally tired and having household chores to take care of creates tensions that can lead to marital conflict. On the other hand, having a spouse who does not work at the plant and who has no idea about the nature of assembly-line work might create a rupture inside the couple on a long run. Jane explains: "My husband gets a little fussy because I get sore. My body hurts, and he thinks I am lazy when I cannot do all the chores around the house." The same story is told by Jim:

I've been through a divorce. I worked in here twelve to fourteen hours and I would go home and still do groceries, bills, cook, clean. My wife was a stay-at-home spouse and did not understand how tired I am. Many people here marry each other after working together for so many years. It's because they understand each other and don't know what they are going through. We spend more time here than at home with our families. In any situation where you have a lot of men and women working together, at hours when they cannot be at home with their families, there will be a bad divorce rate.

After seven years of working in the same group and two and a half years of dating, one couple married, but their group leader quickly contacted Human Resources to move one of them to another group. The couple agrees with the move because working side by side does not work for them. Thomas comments:

> We spend too much time together. We are together 24/7/365. She has issues with me because I do not have anything to talk to her about, but I talk with others every time. She gets aggravated about that. When I worked first shift, I was a lot more anxious to call her and waiting for her phone calls. I couldn't get enough of her. That's probably a bad thing about working with women. We work around them so much, and we get attached to them, and that's what starts affairs.

The team members do not mind to have a couple working in the same group if there is no sexual content in their daily interactions. In other words, the couple earns the respect of the team if they behave professionally at work with no emotional displays of hugging and kissing. Team leaders also face the challenge of dealing with complicated relationships, and they have to be very careful not to give special privileges to couples (e.g., pairing them together on jobs).

Although Carmen's husband does not work at the plant, she is very proud that he understands how hard this work is. She calls Dwight "her best support system" and says that although she has four children of different ages, she has perfect attendance only because he is so helpful and understanding about her work. Carmen realized that she is not motivated enough to work out at the gym during the day (after 2:00 PM when she wakes up), so Dwight, who works first shift, wakes up at 2:00 AM to pick her up from the night shift, and they go to the gym and work out together until 3:30 AM.[2]

Men and Women at Work and Their Families

One of the leading sources of dissatisfaction at the plant is the lack of time for family life. Surprisingly 43% agree that they are able to maintain a balance between their work and personal lives, while 38% disagree (Kaizen Motors opinion survey 2005). One way to partially explain this is to look at how the female workers manage to balance their lives and handle their busy work schedules.

Linda was pregnant with all of her three kids while she was working on the line. The company policy for pregnant workers is that they can work on the line up to 28 weeks, and then they will be assigned to office work. Because Linda had complications with her second pregnancy, her doctor recommended that she rest more, so she went on medical leave when she was two months pregnant. Beverly, her female team leader, explains that they try to help pregnant women if they are nauseous on the line. When asked if men become frustrated or impatient when their female colleagues have morning sickness or "heavy bellies" and maybe cannot perform to their full ability, Beverly answered with a laugh:

But that happens with men, too. Some days they might not feel too good, if they have a flu or something. Then, the whole team works well together. They

did not complain when Linda got pregnant the third time. They just said: "Here we go again!"

Kim tells us about her experience of being pregnant and working on the line:

It was difficult when I got pregnant. You get very tired, more than normal, but I was in my early forties. They let me have ginger ale to cut the morning sickness, and I sucked up little candies. You can go to alternate work duty if you want to. You don't have to stay on line if you don't want to. I went to alternate work duty when I was six months pregnant, I video-taped some processes and did paperwork, and then I joined a safety group. I worked till I was two more months to go. I was standing on my feet all day, with all the added weight. The noise factor is at high level here, and I was worried of all the chemicals here, too. I was paid for family medical leave and stayed home till I had the baby. It's very hard to adjust when you come back. You have only one week, when you work one hour on and one hour off, and your body hurts. It's like you start it from the very beginning. I came here sometimes only after two hours of sleep if the baby did not sleep through the night. Linda also had all her three babies when she was here. We were joking that we will deliver her children right here on the line.

Kay also recalls the time when she was pregnant and working on the line. She applied for a job as soon as she graduated from high-school, but the hiring process lasted two to three years from the moment she sent her application to work at Kaizen Motors. When she finally got in, she was already pregnant, but that did not stop her from accepting the new job on the line. She remembers being extremely tired when she was pregnant with both of her children. On top of this, her position was on the trim line doing the coupes (that do not have a back door), and she had to climb in over the top of the door, but she did this till she was six months pregnant. She became more emotional because she could not see her husband much, since they worked in opposite shifts. Work on the line, however, was useful for women who wanted to get rid of the baby fat after they came back from the maternity leave. Kim's body adjusted very quickly to the physical work. Although she gained forty-two pounds with the baby, she came back to size eight very quickly.

The relationships between the team members and their children are also a very delicate subject because team members do not get to spend more than two to three waking hours at home. If they commute to and from the plant for one to two hours, it is even less than this. Susan, a first-shift mother, describes how she works her toddler son's needs around her own schedule:

My son goes to daycare here on-site. I like that he does not watch TV and has a regular routine there. We wake up at 4:00 AM and get lunch done before coming here. Then, I get him dressed and brush his teeth while he still sleeps. He continues to sleep in the car, and we drop him off at daycare at 5:30 AM, where they let him sleep till 7:00 AM. Then they eat breakfast and all that.

The situation is even more difficult for parents who work in the night shift, thus having a demanding schedule with their children who go to school in the morning. Vanessa, a night-shift mother has to deal with even more complicated life arrangements:

> I meet with the children only for a half an hour, when they get out of the bus, because then I have to hurry to go to work. I wait for them in the mornings, and go to sleep after they are gone to school. I am a single mom and managed all by myself, but I had a sister that lived with us for two years. They could have got in a lot of trouble, but they didn't. They were straight A students. They did not want to disappoint me, out of respect for me, I guess.

So Vanessa comes back home tired from her night shift at 3:30 AM. She does not go to bed and waits for children to wake up at 7:00 AM, so she can steal another thirty minutes with them. It's a total of sixty minutes per day spent with the children, and during this time, the family has some meals together and maybe does homework together.

Dealing with these demanding schedules is very difficult, but none of these mothers showed any signs of bitterness or discontent in their facial expressions or emotions while they were telling their family stories. On contrary, they radiated optimism, dynamism, and laughter around them. They did not dramatize much on this issue or pretend that they are facing impossible demands. Their attitude could be mostly paraphrased as follows: "we are active women with active lives and we are proud that we can provide for our families. Life is life, and we have to deal with it the best we can." However, these tough schedules might work as a disincentive for night shift women to have children. Mary tells us:

> I admire the women that work here and have families. I respect people who do it, but work in the second shift is part of the decision not to remarry and have children. It will take me a decade to get in the first shift. We are told that we may even retire from the second shift.

When team members remarry, they are more likely to form larger and blended families. Most of the team members studied had between two to four children from previous relationships. One female worker said that she now has seven children (three from her husband's first marriage, three from her first marriage, and one common child). With time pressures upon her, she efficiently organized her house work, packed lunches, did the laundry, and took her kids to soccer games. Doing this for seven kids before and after coming to work is obviously tough.

In fact, it is impossible for single mothers, so most of them confessed that they could not work at Kaizen Motors without help from their families. When they go to work, their children are watched by a family member who moves in with them or they spend their time with grandparents. These time pressures also lead to "assembly line childcare," meaning that children are sent from aunts, to uncles, to cousins, to neighbors, or to grandparents, (Hochschild, 1997). The increased demands of high performance work can also drag workers in a third shift, an emotional shift of family crises, neglected children, and divorces (Hochschild, 1997).

Divorce at Kaizen Motors

The divorce rate at Kaizen Motors has been reported as being quite high, and we find that there can be three different paths toward divorce (see Figure 4.1). These processes are outlined with the three underlying causes being (1) the stresses of working on the line with extensive overtime causing family stress and strain; (2) teamwork that involves intense interaction at work and may lead to dating; and (3) the liberating effect of working in a male occupation that pays high wages. The first causal path focuses directly on work pressures creating a strain on the family (3→6→7 in Figure 4.1). Team members at Kaizen Motors spend about sixty hours a week working, and after taking out preparing for work, commuting to work, and sleeping, they have Sunday as their day off and about three and a half hours a day to eat, shop, and spend time with their spouse and family. Five to ten years of this direct pressure will put a strain on any family.

The second path goes through the intense interaction that takes place at work for the sixty hours a week that men and women team members are there. This work intensification leads to very close relationships and dating at work (3→4→5→7). When you spend twice as much time with co-workers (sixty hours) than you spend with your wife or husband (about thirty hours), the former relationship may intensify, while the other fades. With some women going through identity transformations due to lost weight and increased attractiveness, there is a powerful incentive for work-related romances. These romances then lead to marital discord and divorce.

The third path indicates that the empowerment of women may directly or indirectly lead to marital conflict. This may happen to wives who go from low wage jobs to high wage work at Kaizen with corresponding improvements in their self-image. In marriages that are generally strong, this change in roles (i.e., role reversals where women make more than their husbands) may diminish some men's sense of status. While many men can handle a more equal marriage, other men may have great difficulty with these changes. In either case, there is pressure on the marriage, and this may be represented by an indirect path (4→6→7).

In marriages where women were essentially trapped in economically dependent and unsatisfactory relationships, work at Kaizen Motors offered the opportunity of escape. This may be represented by the direct path (4→7) in which the strain in the marriage has always been there and working at Kaizen Motors did nothing to cause their problems. These marriages are a mistake in the first place and these women now have the power to escape them. Kaizen Motors

Figure 4.1: Work related factors that impact family breakup

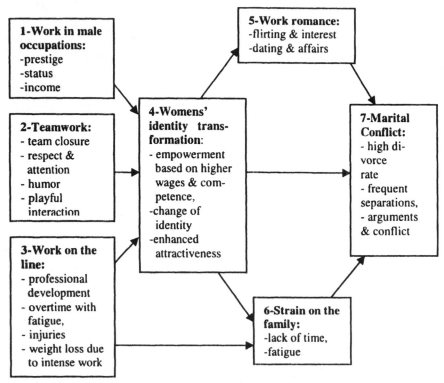

offers an environment in which women have the respect and opportunities to succeed in career like any of their male colleagues. This makes women feel more secure in their future and more confident in their capabilities of taking care of themselves and their children. Consequently, they leave bad and sometimes abusive relationships. Many women interviewed in this project were raised in homes with family values that enforce the traditional gender roles of men being the providers and women being the homemakers. Some of their marriages were quite oppressive and worthy of escape. As a result, martial conflict and divorce may be the result of three very different factors: two related to very long work hours, and one related to empowerment.

Conclusion

This chapter on sexual attraction and families illustrates three paths to marital conflict and possible divorce. First, men and women working in a lean production environment frequently have mandatory overtime, which leads to physical and mental exhaustion. This puts a strain on the family since husbands and wives have little time to spend on family necessities (i.e., shopping, fixing meals, etc.), paying attention to their children, and socializing with friends and relatives. For many workers at Kaizen time pressures are such that social activities are restricted to one day a week (i.e., usually Saturday night). This leads directly to strains on the family.

Second, both women and men may be affected by team intensification of working with members of the opposite sex for long hours in an intense environment. This creates bonds between men and women that can lead to marital problems in their families. The empowerment and gender transformation of women, the mandatory overtime that maximizes contact between team members, the difficulties involved with maintaining a family and marriage with such a demanding job, and the close interactions facilitated by teamwork have led to a high rate of divorce in a long run. The gender transformations with empowerment and attractiveness lead to married team members dating other team members. Pre-existing strains of the job and subsequent relationship difficulties due to long hours of overtime and dating lead to marital breakups. The impact on families, marriages, and dating is an effect of teamwork that is never mentioned in the literature on teams, and this longitudinal effect of teamwork was exposed in this study because the sample included teams with long tenure, sometimes more than a decade.

Third, many women go through an identity transformation at Kaizen Motors and their relationships with their spouses may change. As some of them bring in more money than their husbands, or at least equal amounts of money, the power balance in many marriages may change. Women at Kaizen Motors feel empowered because of their weight loss, their high wages, the self-esteem that they receive resulting from doing well in a "man's world," and the respect and attention that they receive from their male co-workers. As a result, their individual identities are strongly female, but their group identity strongly favors their teams, which constitute and consume so much of their lives.

Thus, there are three paths to higher marital conflict that leads to tensions and eventually divorce. The team intensification theory works well for the very reason that it fell out of favor in the general race relations literature. Lean production teams put people, who are often perceived as different, together with equal status, interlink them in tasks with strong institutional legitimacy, while at the same time achieving a successful outcome recognized by all. With strong management support, team work in lean production fits the contact hypothesis perfectly. As a result, men and women most often stressed their team identities and generalized others over gendered others within the plant. At the same time, women's self confidence and individual identities were clearly strengthened.

The other two theories do not connect to marital conflict. Ely and Thomas' theory of perception and learning has little or nothing to do with it. Kanter's theory about greater numbers of women producing a more equal environment only weakly connects with marital conflict. Conceivably, fewer women in the workplace could produce more pressure on the family, but it seems to be more directly due to the work intensification of the lean production process itself. Neither theory says much about dating at work or gender transformations.

Chapter 5

THE COLOR OF THE LINE: RACE AND IDENTITY IN TEAMS

It is easier to shy away than to talk about it. It is easier for us to pretend it does not exist. We also do it with age and gender. Of course . . . we see color. . . . We just don't want to admit it.   *White team leader*

It is not true that they do not see color. The first thing that you know about every person before if they are cute or ugly, women or men is the color of the skin. It is automatic, instinctive. This is our thought process, the way our society taught us. I like to look at a color quality society, not color blind society.
African American team leader

If you look at the statistics you will find a lot more black women than white women as factory workers. That's because black women are a lot stronger, and we don't have as many options. Many of us are single parents, and we have to feed our kids. We are determined!   *African-American team member*

What are the shop floor interactions between team members of different races and ethnicities at Kaizen and its suppliers? Minority workers' experiences on the line, their contributions to the team efforts, and white co-worker's perceptions of minority workers are a bit more mixed than the women's experiences. Our sociological analysis focuses on emotions generated by the racial interactions, identity transformation of Kaizen minorities and the significance of humor in the lives of teams.

Research on the relationship between race and team performance is limited. Many companies do not want to question the fact that racial diversity might not lead to increased performance, and if they are interested in finding more on this topic, they are not open to allowing independent researchers to study this potentially explosive issue. There are very few studies in the current literature on teams that approach the impact of race and ethnicity on team performance (Kirkman et al., 2004; Timmerman, 2000; Paletz et al., 2004), and most of the research compared African-Americans and whites. Timmerman (2000) found out that age diversity and racial diversity were negatively associated with the team performance of highly interdependent teams (e.g. basketball) and had a null relationship in the case of less interdependent teams (e.g. baseball). The few studies available on this topic reveal that demographic heterogeneity undermines the individual attachment to the group and increases turnover rate (Williams and O'Reilly, 1998; Tsui, Egan and O'Reilly, 1992), leads to increased emotional conflicts in teams (Pelled, Eisenhardt and Xin, 1999), and lowers job satisfaction (Wharton, Rotolo and Bird 2000).

Existing scholarship also points out that racially diverse groups do not necessarily produce a larger quantity of ideas, but they do provide ideas of better quality (McLeod and Lobel, 1996). A recent study observed that although the performance of white teams versus the ethnically diverse teams was equal, the diverse teams reported a more enjoyable working experience with more positive and fewer negative emotions (Paletz et al., 2004).This study, however, shows that racial diversity has a positive impact on team environment and climate as racially diverse teams share a variety of experiences and stories that alleviate the boredom and routine of assembly line work.

Racial Minorities at Kaizen Motors

Past research shows considerable racial segregation in organizational estab-lishments in the US. A black employee is more likely to work in an establish-ment with 35% or more black employees, with this percentage being higher in the small establishments. By contrast, the demographic composition of large companies tends to reflect the demographic composition of the society at around 10-15% (Sorensen, 2004). However, Kaizen Motors does not reflect the same demographic patterns. The demographic composition at Kaizen Motors is 21% female and 79% male, 12% racial minorities of which 10% are African-Americans with 1% are Japanese and less than 1% Hispanic. The total Hispanic population at the plant is 0.81% in the context in which Hispanics have become the largest minority in the US (16% of the total population according to the 2010 US Census). The Hispanic population at Kaizen is underrepresented because first of all, employment at Kaizen Motors is open only for permanent residents and citizens; secondly, some of them do not succeed in passing the hiring tests because of a poor mastery of English language. Most Hispanic workers who work in the factory occupy custodial or contract jobs, which means that they are not Kaizen employees. Kaizen Motors does not sponsor work visas or green-cards, consequently closing the door to many diverse potential employees.

The Kaizen sample included 87 team members: 74 white and 13 minority workers. The minority workers were composed of 11 African-American workers (two women and nine men, representing 12.6% of the sample), one Hispanic male (he identified himself as being Hispanic, although in fact he was biracial and did not speak Spanish), and one Asian (Middle Eastern) male. Out of the 11 African-American workers, three held team leader positions and one was a group leader.

A career at this top global company offers a unique exposure to diversity for native white and black workers. During their tenure at Kaizen Motors, team members worked in the same team with workers from Puerto Rico, Indonesia, Albania, Korea, Sudan, Jordan, Egypt, and Palestine. The initial contact with the Japanese trainers exposed the American workers to different work habits, communication styles, and work ethics. Then, the trips to Japan were a cultural experience that many of the domestic workers will never forget. In addition to the new skills and training that they received at the home company, the white workers had for the first time the chance to experience what it is like to be a minority. These experiences are used as a starting point in their on-site diversity training. Gary, an African-American worker who went to the Japan, recalls:

> When I went to Japan in 1989, the young people will talk to you, but the people in their 60s will not even talk to us and look at us. I was sitting in the subway, and a girl is looking at me. She is pointing at my eyes because they were green. This was the most bizarre feeling I ever had. In the plane in Tokyo, I was that much taller than everybody else. Our guys had scratches on their head because everything was so much shorter on the line in Japan.

Racial Interactions in Teams

Unlike the first two quotes of this chapter, almost all the other team members publicly expressed that they embrace a color-blind perspective. For example, many of them insisted that they do not see color in the daily interactions with their colleagues: "I don't see him (my team mate) as a black man, I see him as Bryan." The white workers insisted that the minority workers are not different in any way than the rest of the workers. The same perspective is embraced by the minority workers themselves who claimed that if they are different from the other workers, it is because of their upbringing and educational background, and not necessarily because of their race. Andrew, a white worker, comments on the theme of color-blindness in teams:

> Everybody is the same. You are here because you have to build that car. You don't really see color when the line is running. When the line is running, there's no diversity. Diversity is only when the line stops, and people break up in their little groups.

And Jack, another white worker, explains that "They [minorities] are pretty much like everybody else. No unique contributions." We can view these comments through four theoretical lenses.

The Team Intensification Theory. The team intensification theory is particularly helpful in explaining how the color-blind perspective is generated by groups. In one of the classical works of social psychology, Allport (1954) found that the level of prejudice between whites and African-Americans is significantly reduced through close contact between these two ethnic groups. But intergroup prejudice is only reduced under specific conditions: (1) close and frequent contact (e.g. residential or occupational contact, not causal contact); (2) equal status of the members of the group; (3) pursuit of common objectives; (4) absence of competition between groups; and (5) authority supporting or enforcing the contact.

As one of the most enduring theories in social psychology, the contact aspect of team intensification theory is largely supported by the existing empirical research (Schiappa et al., 2005; Pettigrew and Tropp, 2006), but it had its share of criticisms. This theory was blamed for analyzing primarily the contact between whites and blacks, while other racial groups are neglected, and for including subjects that have some contacts with other groups, whereas the most racially intolerant individuals do not engage in contact with other races at all (Powers and Ellison, 1995). However, the team intensification theory assists us in explaining the color-blind attitude of teams, as Kaizen teamwork meets all the ideal conditions of intergroup prejudice reduction. First of all, teamwork allows diverse groups of workers to have a close and frequent contact with each other at work. Team members form a group of peers with equal status, who interact on a daily basis on a common project at work. The Kaizen way does not stimulate competition between teams or groups, while the teamwork philosophy along with the ideals of inclusion, tolerance, and respect for people are strongly enforced by Kaizen management.

The Kaizen plant teams are superb examples of the team intensification theory in action. The longer team members work together, the more they develop a tight bond, a sort of brotherhood that over the years moves from the reduced prejudice stage to color-blindness. Team intensification theory does not dismiss our initial theoretical perspectives on diversity, but it rather completes it. Ely and Thomas' study is a cross-sectional study of three different organizations and did not analyze the longitudinal effects of the integration-and-learning perspective of teams. The team intensification theory informs Ely and Thomas (2001) in that if all the afore-mentioned conditions of optimal contact are met, the integration-and-learning perspective of teams is gradually transformed over the years into a color-blind perspective.

The Integration-and-Learning Perspective. The three perspectives in Ely and Thomas' study—integration-and-learning, access-and-legitimacy and discrimination-and-fairness—were generated from workers in a number of departments (which the authors called "work groups"), which did not expose workers to the level of interdependence, synergy and intimacy that are present in Kaizen teamwork. Further, Ely and Thomas' sample was only made up of a third of support staff and two thirds middle and senior managers. It is very likely that the prevalence of managers in the sample altered the findings of the study because these managers were probably more sensitive to the implications of cultural and racial differences than assembly-line workers. Also, the integration-and-learning perspective was analyzed in the context of a law firm, which was a small, non-profit public-interest law firm whose mission is to represent the rights and well-being of economically disadvantaged women. The social mission of this organization to serve the rights of the disadvantaged stimulated the inclusion of the minority staff's perspectives in the core functions of the organizations. When we try to apply the integration-and-learning perspective to the field of manufacturing, the standardized nature of assembly line work and of teamwork leads to the leveling and assimilation of differences, but it does not lead to any particular advantage for African-Americans as it did in Ely and Thomas' study.

Workers at Kaizen Motors were asked to recall their experiences working in all white teams versus their experiences of working in racially mixed teams. They all state that there is no difference. Team members also say that it does not make any difference for them if they have a white or a minority group team leader. This color-blind perspective seems to contradict the integration-and-learning assumptions of Ely and Thomas (2001) as white team members do not report any unique contributions that minority workers bring to the table, while the minority workers themselves confirm that they do not bring anything unique that a white worker does not bring to work. Despite all these limitations of the Ely and Thomas' study, the authors offer plausible evidence indicating how the adoption of the discrimination-and-fairness perspective leads to a colorblind attitude from all the organizational employees, including people of color. The culture of this particular organization was predicated on two norms: conflict avoidance, especially with employees of color, and assimilation to the white cultural standard. However, this colorblind attitude is more a superficial or rhetorical attitude, since this consulting firm is ridden by racial tensions. Whites adopting this perspective were "afraid to recognize that there are differences in culture", and consequently, the minority workers typically did not express their cultural differences (Ely and Thomas, 2001).

For African-American workers, it was hard to name something unique or different that they bring to the table in their teams. African-American workers could not think of something that they bring to a team that a white does not bring. If the colorblind whites could be blamed for ignoring a central part of the identity of their team members of other races and ethnicities, the minority workers themselves seem to be adopting the same colorblind perspective, showing that teamwork indeed levels differences.

The racial dynamic of teamwork at Kaizen Motors shows interesting patterns. For many of the team members, work at Kaizen Motors is a diversity lesson in itself. Workers meet people from across the whole state, of all colors, of different sexual orientations, and of a wide range of ages. They work together in teams and groups and come a long way from their initial fears of diversity to attitudes of color-blindness. The data show that even the minorities who came into teams with a cultural centrist attitude end up being assimilated by the main culture. First shift teams with longer longevity at Kaizen show an even greater attitude of general color-blindness largely brought about by the contacts of team intensification and to some degree by formal diversity programs. Anderson, who is white, asserts:

> Some black people are very sensitive, hyper alert of being black, but after being here for a while, they don't care anymore. We've all been friends here for so long, it does not matter if somebody is black or not.

Nelson comments:

> I am looking at you like a person, not at your sex, race etc. I don't really care if somebody is a minority or not. If you are a good worker, I don't care how you look like. Our core group of people has been here nine to ten years. We've known each other very well. You know what to say and what you cannot say to make one mad. It's very cool that we get along so well.

Graham seconds Anderson's position:

> We are pretty much all the same, other than the color of the skin. I don't see anything, not one thing! I would rather see my children bringing home someone from another race that treats them well than from the same race that treats them bad. It's interesting. That's what kept me in the group for so long. They are so different, so many things to talk about. We have people from across the state of different colors and religions, and we come together so nicely, going to parties to each other places. . . . It's strange that we actually like each other so much.

Racist Beginnings. Many of the white team members at the Kaizen plant have rural backgrounds with very limited opportunities to meet people of color, whereas most of the minorities have a predominantly urban upbringing. Some white workers confessed that they come from families who hold racist attitudes, and their family of origin would not accept their bringing home a spouse of a different color. Therefore, in the beginning, the many white team members had to try hard to fight against their own prejudices. Their initial attitudes were of fear of a different other, and some of them gradually changed to acceptance and even attraction towards these different others. Bradley relates:

> I am from a rural area, and [there is] a lot of discrimination toward women, gay people, black people over there. . . . I have a farming background. My county had very few African-Americans in it. It's not that I did not like them, but I was scared being around them. Right now I do not even think about it.

Robby comments on the same topic: "My dad never liked black people. My uncle said: "You work at Kaizen after they [the Japanese] bombed us!" I said: "Dude . . . that was long time ago!"" These statements are difficult to evaluate without further questions about each persons' deeper attitudes toward race. One suspects that there may be more going on under the surface, which leads us to the next theory.

Symbolic or Aversive Racist Theory. Symbolic racism (Bonilla-Silva, 2006; Bonilla-Silva et al., 2004) and aversive racist theories (Dovidio et al., 2005) view whites' claims of racially neutral environments with great suspicion. In the post-civil rights era, direct racial statements are normatively punished, and in work situations, especially like Kaizen Motors, they can be direct grounds for being fired. Consequently, the vast majority of people say that race does not make a difference to them and performance is what counts. But one white and one African-American worker uncovered some deeper attitudes. Jason, a white team leader, tries to explain the color-blind attitude of his team:

> It is easier to shy away than to talk about it [race or color]. It is easier for us to pretend it does not exist. We also do it with age and gender. Of course . . . we see color. . . . We just don't want to admit it.

Some minority workers do not agree that their colleagues are color-blind. The innocent teasing about someone's race or culture is a proof that race and ethnicity is not an invisible dimension. Roderick, an African-American team leader explains:

> It is not true that they do not see color. The first thing that you know about every person before they are cute or ugly, women or men, is the color of the skin. It is automatic, instinctive. This is our thought process, the way our society taught us. I like to look at a color-quality society, not color-blind society.

But we would like to dig deeper into behavior and social attitudes in their interaction patterns. On the first issue of behavior, we found that interracial teams stuck together on breaks, lunch and so forth. There was no black section of the cafeteria as Bonilla-Silva found in university dormitories and cafeterias. We even have an African-American who said that once one ventured outside of ones team groups, they could not assume that any racial solidarity existed.

In terms of dating there also was no firm color line, and many interracial dates and a few marriages occurred. Terry comments about her attitudes towards a particular black man:

> I am from the country side, pretty back woods. I never thought that I will consider a black man being attractive, but I met a guy on power train who is perfect. He is beautiful, awesome. If he wasn't married, I would date him.

Tina worked as a temp at Kaizen for three years and now works for a supplier because there is less overtime and the work is less hectic. As a black woman, she said that there was a considerable amount of interracial dating that went on at Kaizen Motors.

Symbolic racism theory could also see statements of racial neutrality as evidence of avoidance of "the number-one problem" facing the US today. However, we may ask if this is a fair test of racism. If one worked for a company that failed to employ more than a few African Americans, while 15% of the area was African-American, then the profession of race neutrality would ring false. However, where there is a proportional number of African American employees and an even higher percentage of African American as managers, then professions of race neutrality would seem to be closer to the truth.

On the other hand, there is a small number of white male workers who directly complained about favoritism toward African-Americans, and this is not surprising given the general orientation of the region (e.g., it favored McCain over Obama in the last election and Tea Party sympathies are common). There also were some borderline jokes. One could argue that these workers are asserting white male privilege in these infrequent moments. However, these occurred in a small number of situations with only a few white men in one unit.

However, the presence of this color-blind attitude among the minority workers could be explained in a different way by Kanter (1977b) as an effect of their near token status. The color-blind attitude may contribute to the apparent disconnectedness of African-American workers from each other. Minority workers say that they do not have a preference, and that it does not make any difference for them to have whites on their team. They also do not report that they automatically develop friendships or socialize with members of the same race at work. The enhancing of differences, visibility and tightened control from the majority leads people in the token status to avoid associating with similar others. Also, the research shows that underrepresented minorities exhibit less racial solidarity than the members of the majority (Ibarra, 1995). Team members who had the chance to work with more African-American workers in the same group or team noticed that the black workers tend to have more conflicts with one another than with the White colleagues. Jack, an African-American worker, said that he used to say "Hi" to other black workers at the plant, but he stopped after awhile because they did not reply back. Consequently, he stopped believing that he can develop friendships solely based on race. Jack's current wisdom is that: "Just because we have the same skin tone that does not mean that we have the same culture. Really we don't. We really don't. I never try to make this assumption."[1] On the other hand, there are plenty of African-American workers at Kaizen Motors who are friends with each other.

Kaizen Motors is not a social movement fighting for racial equality at the national level like Ely and Thomas' legal firm. It is a company that enforces a policy of strongly hiring, supporting, and promoting female and African-American workers, and the workers' profession of a racially neutral environment in "their own and frequently mentioned words" generally has credence. This does not mean that all underlying racism has been eliminated, but that in the conduct of the work at hand, performance is what matters. A small number of workers would appear to harbor symbolic racial resentments about promotions, giving some evidence of their feelings that "white privilege has been abridged." But the vast majority of workers indicated that they spent their long days laboring together based on each other's performance rather than race.

Language

Language emerged as a significant dimension in some studies, but there are few, if any, language barriers in this study because employment at Kaizen Motors is only available to US citizens and permanent residents. Therefore, this is not a workplace that is a haven for illegal immigrants. Team members (including the Hispanic team leader) considered that Hispanic immigrants would have a hard time passing the hiring tests because of the language proficiency that is required. However, the outside contractors and the suppliers with whom the Kaizen workers interact on a daily basis have a larger Hispanic workforce.

One of the foreign-born interviewees said that she could not pass the initial hiring tests although she lived in the country more than fifteen years. She thought that she might improve her English if she went to college. After she received her Associate Degree, she was able to pass the Human Resources tests and secure her employment at the plant. This story has larger implications. Since Hispanic workers are under-represented in the plant at less than 1% of all employees, Kaizen Motors should make more efforts to increase their numbers. The access of the Hispanic community to Kaizen plant could be facilitated by the alternative of taking the hiring tests in Spanish, but whether that may happen is an open question.

One team recalled an instance when a Mexican temp joined their ranks. They got along very well with him because he was teaching the team members some Spanish, while the full-time workers taught him English. Other older team members recalled the early phase of the plant when the Japanese trainers came everyday on the shop floor. The American workers were almost nostalgic remembering how helpful the Japanese trainers were despite their language barriers.

Language is also mentioned in the interactions between White and African-American team members. A white member preferred to have a black team leader because he speaks in a more informal way than his previous white leaders. However, Randall, an African-American group leader, mentioned that he is conscientiously trying not to talk in African-American slang with the other black members of his team as he wants to approach all his subordinates in the same way. Randall says:

> I cannot treat my black team leaders with phrases that I do not use around other team leaders. How can I say: "What's up, big dog" when I talk to a female team leader?

Joking and Difference

Since Kaizen Motors' diversity training film warns against joking about race, ethnicity and gender; joking is a sub-current at Kaizen Motors. One African-American woman in the paint shop and one African-American man on the assembly line reported that they never joked about race. But humor can offer relief from the monotony and tyranny of the line. Some white workers say that it is more interesting to be on diverse teams because, as John puts it:

> Joking is extremely important at work. We would lose our minds without it. You have to joke! I hated it the first time when nobody was joking with me. I hated walking in here every day. Once you get people joking with you, it's a huge difference. Sometimes the older team members joke even more, actually.

Thus, joking (including some of its more negative forms of teasing and hazing) may be a ritual of inclusion and initiation that transforms the "different other" into a "generalized other." Joking can be the first step and ultimate proof of the integration and adaptation of differences at the team level.

Diversity can also be considered a significant factor that contributes to workers' well-being, since humor and joking are used as a protective shield from the numbness and routine of the line. In an industry with a high rate of safety hazards and risks, situational and coping humor indirectly improves workers' morale, health and psychological well-being (Simon, 1990; Martin et al., 1993). Humor and laughter trigger our natural painkillers (endomorphins), which in turn help us to adapt to and diffuse stressful situations and reactions (Berk, 1989; Weisenberg et al., 1995; Thorson and Powell 1997; Parrish and Quinn, 1999; Garrick, 2006). Humor as a form of emotion work is often times mobilized in occupations with increased levels of emotional stress: soldiers (Le Naour, 2001), care givers (Parrish and Quinn, 1999), and police officers (Martin, 1999). Thus, diversity sparkled with humor can be a coping and therapeutic strategy for dealing with stress with an indirect and positive effect on team performance.

Although an indispensable dimension of the life on the line, joking can become a double-edge sword when race and ethnicity comes under fire. Racially and ethnically insensitive jokes are not welcome. The topics of jokes that touch upon race are: workers' backgrounds ("inner city boys" versus "hillbillies"); food preferences (hamburgers versus fried chicken and neck-bones); past careers, families and children; and sports (e.g. whites playing basketball or African-Americans trying golf).

In these situations, the cultural differences are very subtle. All the team members agreed that they know their colleagues for such a long time that nobody is offended when jokes touch the issues of race or culture. However, some white team members really worried about what the other races might think about their jokes. They wondered if these jokes were too sensitive for the minority workers, but they noticed that none of the facial expressions, gestures or behavior of the minority workers showed that they are upset. Some team members totally avoided joking about race since they have trouble reading cues as to whether the target of the joke feels uncomfortable or not.

When people recall their experiences with working side by side with foreign-born team members, they noticed that these workers "do not have the same sense of humor that Americans have" and sometimes do not understand the meaning of the jokes. However, workers do not understand that this is not a matter of having a good sense of humor or not, but it relates back to the language barrier. Foreign-born team members are also reported to be very sensitive about jokes about their country or cultures and to take it very personally if they do not get the joke. For instance, the Middle Eastern worker was teased by his colleagues that they are going to call airport security and warn them that there is an Arab guy coming in. He replied laughing: "No bother, guys, airport security will stop me anyway!" In other groups, he was told to go back where he is from, or co-workers made fun of him that he is a camel-rider. He laughed at such comments because he came to US when he was a toddler and never saw a camel. He actually considers himself an American with an Arab name.

If the foreign-born seem to lack some sense of humor, the domestic minorities, mostly African-Americans, are described most often as "the ones who crack jokes" and "hilarious" with the "craziest sense of humor." Team members started to become more comfortable about joking about race after they noticed that the minority workers joke about their color themselves. Anthony, a white worker, says:

> When our team took a picture together, somebody said: "Make sure you use the flash for John!" and then I said: "John, you are that black spot in the corner with the white teeth." He laughs. He likes it. He thinks it's funny. He said: "That is the good-looking one over there!" We are all friends and feel comfortable with each other. It is not an issue. I've never been in a place like this. You walk out of here and it is totally different. Race starts to be a problem. Here people are persons, not black guys, or Hispanics.

When we talked to John about this incident, he says that he remembers the joke. "I might smile, and I am coming back and say something to you. It is no biggie to me. I am not ashamed of what color I am."

But when jokes go awry, both whites and blacks express regrets. Aaron, a white team member painfully remembers one incident:

> We had a diversity hat day. The whole thing is funny anyway, because we can wear only bobcats. We were talking about Mexican hats. At home I have a Robin Hood costume, and I said: "Can we include hoods?" The group leader gave me those looks. It was so horrible. I felt so bad. . . .

Aaron recounts John's reaction: "Thank God, John knows me and said: 'I know what you meant, man!'" As we can see, John was the target of at least two racial jokes, which apparently contradict the color blind attitude. The big question is: Is racial humor an integration and adaptation strategy (Ely and Thomas, 2001), or a social and psychological distancing technique from workers of different races?

There are two major scenarios that explain why the minority workers are not offended by the racial jokes and even encourage them. The integration and adaptation scenario uses the assumption that humor is an integration technique.

In this case, the minority workers are not only integrated, but also assimilated into the team culture. Minority workers adopt a color-blind perspective and are not offended by the racial jokes because they see themselves as team members. The symbolic interactionist scenario would say that teams have their own feeling and emotion rules (Hochschild, 1979), meaning that team members should be collegial and not get offended, even when humor touches the hot topic of race. Thus, the acceptance of joking has become an informal group norm. Symbolic interactionist theory emphasizes the importance of meanings associated with the social interactions. Is the meaning of racial jokes in this case a cohesive or divisive agent of teams? We believe that it is mostly cohesive, but when it verges on being divisive, team members apologize to each other.

Joking on gender, age, race or sexual orientations reveals an awareness of differences or different generalized others. As a central dimension of team and group interactions, humor triggers in these circumstances mostly positive emotions. This is another example that casts doubt on the concepts of shame, embarrassment and stigma as the dominant emotions of these social interactions. Joking in teams is most often associated with feeling comfortable, and having fun together rather than with embarrassment, fear, anger, or resentment. Joking and humor in teams was not included in our initial hypotheses, but it was identified by team members as a fundamental dimension of work in a team. However, these interviews cannot be conclusive on the nature of racial jokes in groups. Further investigation is needed to conclude how racial joking coexists with a presumably color-blind perspective, how comfortable minorities are with racial joking, as well as to what extent minorities initiate similar forms of teasing with their white co-workers.

Favoritism

A small number of workers reported that there is favoritism for workers of color at the plant. Both white and minority workers prove in this context that they misunderstand and misinterpret the principles of affirmative action, equal employment, and diversity at work. Some of them suspected that the company has to meet a certain quota of minorities at the plant, but they blame the government rather than the company for this situation. Some white team members consider that minority workers can pass the employment tests easier than the white workers because they receive extra points solely for their minority status. Other workers believe that if a black worker is in the position to be promoted, he or she would be picked over the white worker with the same record. One worker called this affirmative action policy a form of reverse discrimination, while others called it being "politically correct." A worker recalls working with a black team member who made a lot of mistakes in his work, and at one point, when he drove the forklift, had an accident destroying $100,000 worth of parts. He was not reprimanded and still drives the forklift, which the worker thinks would not have had happened if he had been white. Favoritism is blamed again in the following case in which Johnson, a white team member, comments:

It took me three years to move to the first shift. For a black guy it took three months to get here. Some people that were hired after me advanced quicker than me because of color. How could they do that? I have a technical background. They flipped burgers before they came in here. I just don't get it.

However, only a few white workers complained about favoritism. The perception from these interviews is that the African-American workers might be on a "glass escalator" at Kaizen Motors. The glass escalator, which is opposite the concept of a glass ceiling, represents the structural advantages and privileges that some groups have in advancing their careers (Williams, 1992). However, this perception is not confirmed by the company data that show that only 10.7% of African-Americans hold leadership positions. The mere presence of a minority person in a leadership position makes some whites ignore the possibility that they themselves might not be qualified for the job or promotion (Bonilla-Silva et al., 2004). Complaints against the affirmative action policies are common forms of symbolic or aversive racism. These new forms of covert or modern racism include surprise and envy on the minority success. The complaints about the promotion of minority workers are examples of a few whites not actually being ready to give up their feelings of white privilege.

Minority workers do not accept the same perception of favoritism. They believe that as minority workers they do not have more opportunities than whites at Kaizen Motors. But they do have equal chances just like everybody else. Some white workers do not shy away from directly blaming minorities for accepting preferential treatment. Whitney, a black team member, explains in an interview: "You have to work hard to meet the quota [of blacks]. Quotas will not hurt. It is to my benefit. I am not sure if the whites are not jealous" of the opportunities that blacks have.

Two or three white workers noticed instances when some minority workers use the race card to threaten the company with a racial discrimination lawsuit if they were fired. In one instance, even when a black team leader recommended the firing of one of his black subordinates, that person still claimed that it was racial discrimination. Some team members believe that the Human Resources Department is scared of reprimanding minority workers even when they have good reasons to act (e.g., poor attendance or performance).

Workers believe that harassment in general (racial or sexual) is the easiest way of losing employment at Kaizen Motors. Poor performance on the job does not carry such a harsh penalty as the racial harassment. Kaizen workers related an incident when some slurs were written on the walls in the bathroom, and the company immediately made some announcements that this type of behavior is not going to be tolerated.

Experiences of African-American Workers

Kaizen Motors Annual Opinion Survey offered valuable quantitative data to back up the qualitative data obtained through the interviews. The annual opinion survey was filled by almost a half of Kaizen Motors' total workforce, and helps us draw a general picture of minority workers' experiences on the line. The final results show that the Asian employees hold more favorable opinions about their work at Kaizen Motors in general (they hold top management positions generally associated with higher job satisfaction). Another significant pattern is that African-American workers record higher satisfaction scores than the white workers on all the survey items, which makes them appear to be the most satisfied racial group. Hispanic employees only score higher than white workers on a few items since their custodial positions at the bottom of the organizational hierarchy have lower status, opportunities for professional development, and access to teamwork.

The following interviews shed some light on why the African-American group is the most satisfied racial group at Kaizen Motors. First of all, some African-American workers feel that they have a deeper connection to teamwork. African-American workers believe that cooperative work is an important part of the African-American heritage. A black worker noticed that in the history of slavery, African-American people had to work together, rely on each other, and make sacrifices for one another, thus having a historical connection to the principles of teamwork and inclusion.

A black team leader describes his experience of leading a team of white men. He was hired at Kaizen Motors at the age of 21 and promoted to the position of team leader two years later. Now, fifteen years later, he remembers how strict his leadership was in the beginning ("I had to be strict, not because I was black, but because I was the youngest in the whole team"). He identifies so much with his work at the auto factory that his friends call him the "Kaizen man." But he tries hard not to put on the "Kaizen face" when he comes to work, and he wants to act the same way with his co-workers and his black friends. He feels proud and unique for being one of the few black leaders on the shop floor, and he makes conscious efforts not "to act white."

Despite the stereotype that minority leaders tend "to take care of their own," black workers feel that black supervisors are tougher on them because they do not want to show any form of favoritism. Therefore, the black team leaders are even more demanding with the black workers. In a quote that seems driven from Kanter's work on tokenism (1997b), Mark, a black team member, says that workers experience more pressure and scrutiny from their black leaders simply because they are black:

> To a degree it hurts to have an African-American team leader. He expects a little bit more from me. He feels that I should go 120% even in my bad days. He is a tough group leader, very direct and pushy, African-American style.

Brad, another black team member, explains why he feels blessed for his job at Kaizen Motors:

> Kaizen presents a lot of opportunity for us. If you look at the outside world, African-Americans do not have any opportunities. Coming here and making the same amount of money as the person next to you and being able to afford the things that you want for your family, you cannot be anything but happy. There are no other better employers in our state. I make a lot more than my other African-American friends. They think I am the luckiest man in the world. You hear things here and there. "He is lazy because he is black." It upsets me, but it only makes me work harder.

Warren, a black group leader, feels that his black friends are envious of him because of his accomplishments at Kaizen Motors. Most of his friends work for one of the Big Three American auto factories but despite the fact that they work in an environment with a higher percentage of minority workers, they would trade their jobs with the Japanese company at any time. Recalling the past, Warren expresses pride in his current position:

> My grandparents had seen people hanging from trees, parts cut up, public lynching at churches. These were my blood. It makes me appreciate what I have today. African-American workers at the Kaizen plant can do everything they put their heart and soul to. We are the internal treasure that Kaizen has. These are the rules, this is the system and you have an equal shot to being promoted. African-American workers are exactly where they choose to be.

Warren went on to say that an American auto company had tried to hire him, and that he chose to stay at Kaizen despite his 80-mile commute.

> I worked 30 years, and this is a company where for the first time in my life I like coming to work. When you come to this door, if you want to make a difference and be successful, you can. . . . If I prove myself, I can smoke anybody. I burn them down the wall. There are companies with a good old-boy network, where you have to know somebody to get promoted, but Kaizen gave me a chance to prove myself.

This African-American team leader is a good example of the coexistence of multiple selves and multiple generalized others. He had developed a "double consciousness" (DuBois, 2005): his African-American heritage encourages him to work for the American auto companies, which traditionally provided employment for many African-American workers, but on the other hand, he has become "the Kaizen man" who internalized profoundly the Japanese culture and philosophy of work.

The community of fate of the Kaizen workers is shown also outside of work, in the social geography of the company town. If employees used to come to work from traditionally white and black neighborhoods or white and black areas of the state, they live now in mixed neighborhoods. One black team member at Kaizen Motors said that he did not even look for houses in the black neighborhood when he decided to settle down in the company town. A Kaizen job brings considerable wealth to an African-American family, so now the surrounding communities do not distinguish themselves by race, but by economics. Thus, the melting pot at work generated a melting pot of races and ethnicities living together in the same neighborhoods in the proximity of the plant. In a few instances, some spouses of the Kaizen workers who were not exposed to diversity to the same extent do not want to leave the predominantly white areas and relocate in the mixed neighborhoods in the company town. At least in one instance, a worker had to drive every day four hours (two hours back and forth) from his small town to the plant because his wife was afraid of living in mixed neighborhoods.

Wilson, the oldest person in the study, was a 61-year old African-American team leader. He started his career at Kaizen Motors at the age of 49, after he retired from the army. Wilson's story is also a touching story of hard work and success, and his destiny is now intertwined with the company:

> Kaizen is a very good company to work for. I have been treated super. You wouldn't understand how it is to be on my side. When I got to school, I had to go cut firewood; I had to work all the time. Kaizen gave African-Americans a better opportunity to reach a goal they never thought they will reach. They can buy a house... it brings wealth to the African-American community. Kaizen gives minorities a chance, that's why they drive a hundred miles. When you start driving that far for a job with the price of gas today, don't tell me that person does not like the job! That speaks for itself. There are promotion opportunities for African-Americans. All you have to do is to stay out of trouble, apply yourself, do what you need to do, and the opportunities are there. Myself with my age, I am a model.

Benecia said that working for Kaizen Motors was great and added that "you have to understand that I was working a minimum wage job and receiving government support for my two children." Quentin, a younger African-American worker, confirms this position toward Kaizen Motors:

> Kaizen took us away from the bad neighborhoods we were living in. It gave us a better outlook on life. Kaizen is not easy, but at the same time, it gives opportunities. A lot of people feel blessed and happy to have this good job.

Some workers believe that diversity is promoted by their company only for public relations purposes or for pressure to conform to governmental regulations. Only one African-American worker used the perfect attendance ceremony as a proof that diversity is a superficial concept at Kaizen Motors: all the groups that sang at the ceremony were country music groups, while only one group was geared towards the African-American audience, and there was no Hispanic band whatsoever. However, music is changed every two hours on the line in order to accommodate a diverse range of musical preferences.

Gendered interactions of African Americans with whites

African-American men, African-American women, and white women are minorities at Kaizen Motors. Obviously, not all racial interactions are between African-American and white men. So this section emphasizes some intersectionality of race and gender interactions. There is some evidence that African-American men are more cooperative with women workers. Jackson, an African-American team member, comments:

> I think women are a little more open to the differences, just because they are more nurturing. They will give people chances. I am more open towards women, to what they have to say. I would like to make their work easier. When a woman is hurt, I like to help her out. This is the way my mom brought me up, to always look out for women. This is part of our African-American culture. We were raised more with our mothers. All we had is our mothers and their protection.

This African-American man says that he is more willing to help women, whereas most of the white men say that they would not help a female team member more than they would a man.

Two African-American team leaders found that they could interact effectively and lead white women and men. George, the African-American group leader, makes sure that he "looks everyone in the eye" and that in solving a nasty dispute that could have ended up in a sexual harassment case, he considered how he would have wanted his daughter to be treated at Kaizen Motors. As a result, he came up with a highly effective way of toning that conflict down (i.e., the T-shirt solution). We do not have a large number of interviews on these interactions, but at least two of the African-American men seemed to be empathetic toward women. And also in Chapter 3, Briona, the female team leader, found that when white men on her team did not listen to her, she told them that "I am the boss, and we all have to keep our jobs." She said that "being an African-American leader" was never an issue for her.

Dating and its impact on families was a major topic in the previous chapter on women, and interracial dating has always been a highly charged topic. It is useful to compare interracial dating at the main Kaizen plant and at many of its supplier firms. The supplier firms consist of greater numbers of younger workers, and they are much more likely to date because they are often single, and they are in the prime of their sexual lives. The main Kaizen Motors plant is generally older, and more of its workers are married.

There is less emphasis on diversity at the supplier firms. While some of the supplier firms hire many African-Americans and some immigrants, there is less corporate support for diversity. As a result, there is sometimes more evidence of role encapsulation. Brenda, a team leader in one of the supplier firms describes how an African-American woman's role can be constrained.

The hardest part of this work is that you don't always get to be pretty. You are
not girlie, you are tomboyish, you look gay. Yah, I've heard it: "You are a les-
bian?" But if you wear a lot of make-up, then you hear that you are a tramp or a
whore. . . .

This is a clear-cut example of Kanter's concept of "role encapsulation" (1977b:
230-38) that comes from a supplier firm, but not from Kaizen itself.

Contributions of minorities

Minority workers bring different perspectives and view points to their
teams, but most of all, they bring different topics to talk about that alleviate the
boredom of the line. Minorities also bring different cultural backgrounds to their
groups. Since the Hispanic minority was severely underrepresented in our sample, we can speak more about the African-American workers and how they fit in
their teams. African-American workers bring a lot of laughter, humor, and re-
laxation, which are indispensable survival strategies of the work on the line.
Fred, an African-American team member, comments:

We talk, joke around. As an African-American, I know how it feels to be down
(especially for temps). The process that temps have to go through is grueling,
and working and not making the same pay. My contribution is to keep everybody's head up. Life is tough. I try to make everybody smile.

Team members' perception is that people of different races and ethnicities
do not bring unique or different contributions to team performance (suggestions
and problem-solving, quality, productivity, and safety). However, minority
workers have a positive effect on the team climate, which is an intermediary
variable leading to team performance. Regarding the team climate, minority
workers agreed that Kaizen is a great employer to work for, a workplace where
they feel valued and respected by their co-workers and supervisors.

Tasha, an African-American female team leader, thinks that her greatest
contribution to her team is the chance to prove to people that African-American
women do not like to sit back and do nothing while "living on welfare," but that
they like to work when they are offered opportunities. All of her team members
are extremely enthusiastic and supportive of their team leader. Alexis praises
Tasha:

We love Tasha to death. She brings something because she is a bubbly person.
She is the highlight of our team. She is energetic; she is laughing and talking,
she is up-beat, always has something to say. She is not afraid to voice herself,
which is good. She is fun to work with.

When team members share their experiences with working side by side with
African-American co-workers, their stories touch the same points: that the Afri-

can-American workers are happier, more relaxed, more talkative, more up beat. Also, African-American workers seem to be more open and supportive towards the newcomers of the group (including temps). Usually they are the first ones to approach the newcomers and to start joking with them, thus initiating them in the team spirit. Most stories involved African-American workers and the central aspect of humor. Jim, a white team member, says that he likes Mark:

> Mark is funny. He dances, he is hilarious, he makes everybody laugh. . . . In this kind of environment, you feed off of this. We are here stuck at night when everybody is sleeping. Oh, my Gosh, he makes you laugh! He . . . lights up a room as soon as he gets in.

Michael, a white team member, comments:

> African-American workers have more humor. They cut up with you more. They crack me up, they pick at you. They made me feel more comfortable. They are the ones that will approach you faster than anybody and have conversation with you. They are the first ones who talked to me, they are more approachable.

Preference for diversity

Although we have no evidence to prove that the performance of diverse teams is higher than the performance of homogenous teams, work is reportedly a more enjoyable and pleasant experience overall in the high diversity teams. Thus, contrary to the previous findings on the potential conflicts that diversity brings to work, diversity at Kaizen Motors leads to a more positive team climate and strengthens the team spirit and morale, both of them being intermediate factors that ultimately lead to higher performance.

Our discussion on diversity comes as a full circle. In the beginning of their careers at the Kaizen plant, team members' attitudes towards diversity were influenced by their families and their backgrounds. After working for more than ten to twenty years at Kaizen Motors, workers bring these enriching experiences on world culture, tolerance, and understanding to their families. The diverse work experience at Kaizen Motors helps employees raise their families in a spirit of mutual understanding of different cultures and ethnicities. These well-rounded children will contribute to the social progress of our future society. And in many work stations throughout the plant, visitors can see posters called "The Diversity Garden" which consists of the photos of children hanging on tree branches along with the children's words describing what they mean by diversity.

Conclusions on Race

This chapter on race and ethnicity at Kaizen Motors has illustrated four major findings. First, most of the workers admired Kaizen for being one of the most diverse companies they have ever worked for and for providing employment opportunities for all the minorities. From the survey data, the minority groups (Asian, African-American, and Hispanic) are surprisingly more satisfied and appreciate their jobs at Kaizen somewhat more than the white workers. From the interviews, Kaizen Company teams adopt a colorblind attitude on racial differences that is better explained by team intensification theory than by Ely and Thomas (2001) where there is a special skill or market connection for minorities. Teamwork offers the optimal conditions for the color-blind attitude to develop and the contact aspect of team intensification theory works. Thus, team intensification theory informs the integration-and-learning perspective of the long-term consequences of a diverse workforce working together.

Second, although the interviews did not reveal a direct link between race and key performance indicators (problem solving, quality, productivity, and safety), racial diversity was discovered to have a positive impact on team climate. Racial and ethnic diversity leads to a more enjoyable and fun experience at work, which is a fundamental dimension of the life on the line.

Third, Kanter's theory about greater numbers of minorities producing a better environment is neither confirmed nor denied. Although the African-Americans, the largest minority group, seem to be disconnected from each other, the interviews and the opinion survey reveal higher feelings of satisfaction and pride at work among these minority members than among the white workers.

Fourth, there are some complaints from a few white workers involving favoritism for minorities. But this was not confirmed by the company data on promotions and leadership among the different minority groups. In a plant of this size, the absolute number of African-Americans group and team leaders was relatively small. So this does provide an explanation of white privilege theory for a small number of white workers. One African-American worker recommended the company to obtain more minority singers at the company reward ceremonies, which seemed to be dominated by country and western bands, but music in the plant covered a much broader array of music.

In the end, however, we must remain somewhat wary of our conclusions and results for African-Americans at Kaizen Motors. Our interviews on company time, in which two African-American workers refused to participate, pose some significant problems concerning "racism without racists" (Bonilla-Silva, 2006; Dovidio et al., 2005). We cannot accept the one-sided evidence from a few white workers who said that those who refused to be interviewed sometimes play the race card as reliable, except perhaps as evidence about what white workers think. And using humor is certainly important in some assembly teams and informal groups of workers. However, humor is certainly not a unique advantage to one group, and it has a perilously close connection to aggression through ethnic or racial jokes. Consequently, we can only conclude what our evidence shows: there are many African-Americans who are promoted to team- and group-leader positions, many African-American workers do well in teams, but there were a small number of African-Americans who refused to talk to us. Those hidden viewpoints might be more negative, but we simply can neither confirm nor deny these contentions.

Additional interviews with African-Americans who were former Kaizen workers showed that one who was injured was highly negative, one who was injured was very positive, and others who were initially wary but then expressed a strong pride in having worked at Kaizen. Walter says: "You know, we know how to do it right!" But exactly those same sentiments were found among whites who were formerly employed at Kaizen. Being injured at work, whether you are white or black, generally does not endear one to the company. It was surprising that one who was injured was not negative.

In sum, most black and white workers gave us race neutral answers, a few black workers said that race was noticed but did not provide any negative behaviors that went with it, a few white workers expressed resentment about blacks being promoted, and a very small number of African-American workers would not talk to us. Aside from two white and two black workers, the vast majority of African-American and white workers seem to get along well with each other, and many of the African-American workers were promoted and proud to work there. In a sense, Kaizen Motors may be similar to the US Military that has a strong support for racial equality going back to President Truman's desegregation order and also an element of working in teams (i.e., squads). A partial explanation given for less racial discrimination and more fraternization among racial groups in the military is that it is a total institution (Lindquist, 2004; Moskos and Butler, 1996). In a sense, Kaizen Motors shares some elements of these team relationships and intense environments with the military services.

Chapter 6

THE AGING GURUS AND YOUNG GUNG-HOES

We do more movements in one day than most people do in a month, so we lose our elasticity in our joints on a long run. They take the easy jobs away. The group absorbs these jobs and it's a little bit faster and faster, and that adds up over the years. I don't know how long I can continue to work like that, if I will grow older here.   *An old team member*

The older are smarter. They go around the block. The younger work the hardest way. The older will tell them: "What are you doing? There's an easier way to accomplish this."   *An older team member*

I would work with older team members because they are more forgiving if you make a mistake. They are more apt to coach and to work with you, to help you learn. They are not in a hurry, you do not feel rushed.

A young team member

Most of the previous studies on the Japanese transplants were about the early phases of lean production. Workers at Japanese transplants have aged since then. This study takes place in the twenty-first century and asks workers about their long-term experiences with lean production and can more effectively explore the link between age and lean systems. The top Japanese transplants did not have lay-offs in their first twenty years of production, and consequently, they demonstrate how lean production copes with an aging workforce.

   In the case of physically demanding jobs, one may argue that age lessens the physical strength needed to perform these kinds of jobs. Younger workers expose on average higher levels of enthusiasm, energy, and physical strength. Older workers show higher levels of motivation and commitment, lower turnover, less absenteeism (Rhodes, 1983), and less adaptability in acquiring new skills and knowledge (Warr, 1995). Age explains little variance in the work performance of teams, partially because the potential negative impact of age is balanced by the potentially positive impact of work experience associated to age (Williams and O'Reilly, 1998; McEvoy and Cascio, 1989; Waldman and Avolio, 1986).

The controversial issue of age is barely mentioned in only two of the early studies of Japanese transplants. At the Mazda plant, Fucini and Fucini (1995) noticed that work intensification leads to early signs of aging and early carpal tunnel symptoms, while a half of the CAMI workers anticipated that if they continue to do the overburdened jobs and work in understaffed teams they will be injured or worn out before retirement (Rinehart et al., 1997).

Figure 6.1: Age distribution of Kaizen team members, 2006

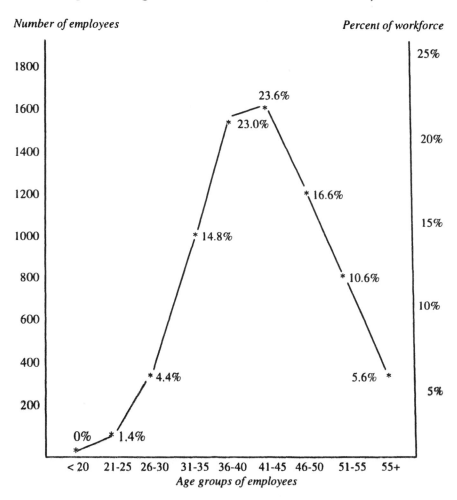

The Kaizen plant hired the majority of its workforce in the late 1980s and early 1990s. Over fifty-six percent of Kaizen employees are over 35 years old and thirty-three percent are over 45 (see figure 6.1). The workers whom we interviewed showed a similar age structure with over sixty percent of the first shift coming from workers aged 35 to 44, while only thirty-six percent of the second shift came from this same age group (see Table 6.1).

In this study, younger workers are defined as workers younger than forty years old and the older workers are forty and over. Although forty years old is the cornerstone for middle age, we consider it old age for assembly line workers who usually develop early signs of aging and retire around the age of 50 years old. Thus, there was only one worker older than 55 on each shift.

Table 6.1: Sample composition by age and shift

Age group	Shift 1		Shift 2	
	Number	%	Number	%
20-24 years old	0	0	4	9.1%
25-34 years old	9	20.9%	17	38.6%
35-44 years old	26	60.5%	16	36.4%
45-54 years old	7	16.3%	6	13.6%
Older than 55	1	2.3%	1	2.3%
Total	43	100%	44	100%

Experiences of Older Workers in Teams

Kaizen teams do not have high age diversity; they are not melting pots of grandparents and kids. On contrary, shift work splits up the Kaizen workforce into two different relatively homogenous age cohorts: first-shift teams average 45 years old, and second-shift teams average 35 years. Both older and younger workers feel valued and respected in their teams regardless of their age. Older workers feel that the younger look up to them and the leadership they can provide. Although younger workers do not have any open criticisms towards the older colleagues in their teams, they are very critical of the people who work on the first shift. The first shift has a poor reputation with slower productivity, which the younger workers blame on the careless attitude of workers with more seniority.

The experiences of older workers are dominated by a feeling of insecurity and incertitude regarding their future at the plant. Most of them could not predict how long they will be able to work at the plant, but all of them were hoping to retire from Kaizen. Older workers' stories gravitate around the main idea that old age and lean production fit together like oil and water. William describes what it is like to be an older worker and to work on the line at Kaizen:

I hope to get some easier jobs. That's what everybody is hoping for. . . . They take the easy jobs away. The group absorbs these jobs, and it's a little bit faster and faster, and that adds up over the years. I don't know how long I can continue to work like that, if I will grow older here. I was talking to the other people, and everybody is complaining about this. When is it going to be enough? When are they going to say that this is an honest day of work? Why should we kill our workforce? It is never enough. If we do 100%, next day we have to do 160 instead of 150 cars.

Team members who worked for more than ten years on the line (some of them in their late thirties and early forties) complained about the wear and tear on their bodies, and wondered how much they could take. They say that it is extremely hard, if not impossible, to last on the line for more than twenty years. A 48-year old worker with only eight years on the line applied for a transfer in an off-line department for less pay only to make his body last longer. Even so, he seriously doubts that he could make his body last seven more years till he reaches fifteen years of service and the age of fifty-five.

Another interview supports the "lean and mean" hypothesis. Older workers describe the difficulty of coping with work intensification and the pain in their joints. Some of them are concerned that the lean line exposes workers to a higher risk of getting injured because they have to rotate the same jobs more often during a shift than they should (in some cases, team members have to do the same job four times instead of only once). A few of Kaizen workers praised the American auto companies, especially Ford, for taking better care of their older workers. Scott wearily states:

A lot of us hope we can make it to the bell. Our jobs are tighter and tighter, faster and faster, harder and harder. We are making some jokes that (lean) is like they cut all the fat, but now it is like they cut all the meat and they are slicing it into the bone. We are wondering if our bodies can take it. There are a lot of people hurt over there. I could not even tighten my boots this morning. My hands pulled off. If you've been with Kaizen over ten years, and you have not been seriously hurt, you're probably going to be. After fifty or sixty, your body does not recover so well from all the damage. Here is twice or three times harder than the plant I worked before. You reach fifty; your body wears out. I have so many injuries on my body I cannot count them. They run this place too lean. Every line is running bare bones, minimum, every man is overburden and everybody is stressed because manpower is so bad. They do not care if you are ninety out here. I don't like it. I hate to see me at fifty-five working here.

One idea that came out from the interviews with the older workers is that the overall society, but particularly a successful company like Kaizen Motors, should find better ways to protect the older workers (e.g., like retirement for police and fire fighters) because, according to most workers, one cannot last on-line for more than twenty-five years. A frequent suggestion is that the easier jobs (mostly the off-line jobs) should be based on seniority, thus geared towards the senior workers. Older workers see themselves as the internal treasure of Kaizen, because they have accumulated an invaluable experience, whereas if Kaizen hires young workers, the company has to use more resources to train them.

None of the older workers we talked to had a clear plan for retirement or vision regarding their post-Kaizen careers. They just pray to be able to work as long as possible at the plant. A 55-year old woman who was injured at work after twelve years on the assembly-line at Kaizen Motors, describes the transitional jobs she took when she came back from restriction. Workers who come back from restriction go through two transitional weeks when they work one hour in and one hour off, then two hours on and two hours off. However, older workers do not heal as fast as younger workers, and they end up going on the line in pain. Donna complains about her hands:

> I just came back from a leave of six months at 60% pay rate [restriction]. It was like heaven. I hope to retire from here, but I don't see it. I try to go year by year; I take a day at a time. By the way, I am glad that this is on tape, maybe somebody will listen to this. My hands are ruined. I cannot even write a letter. I used to write letters to my mom. Now I go on the computer and do my bills online because I cannot even fill a check. I go month by month and year by year, and see how long I can make it. I do what I can to keep the speed, but not the quality. Team members in my team have to pick up my slack. I have to take pain medication. I take double dose at lunch time. I have good days and bad days.

Team leaders mention that sometimes younger workers feel frustrated when the older workers cannot keep up. They were "down" on an older woman because she could not finish a difficult door job in time, but the team leader defended her in front of the team and worked with her to get her back to speed. The team came up with improvements to accommodate her situation—a piece of equipment that carries the heavy parts for her to the next car. Ultimately, these types of improvements help all the team members accomplish their tasks in a more comfortable way. Team leaders are portrayed as being more protective with the older workers. For instance, one of the team leaders says that he is constantly reminding the younger workers that they are going to be old one day. Anderson acknowledges:

> The older workers are much more detailed oriented, more nit-picking in a good way. The younger workers pick up on things a little faster. Older people can be limited physically; it takes longer to learn a job. Younger workers will ask me: "When will John or Helen get better on the job?" I just remind them that one day they will be on the same boat. Attitude makes up for lack of ability. If the attitude is there, the team members will understand. They will help each other out if you have good communication. As a team leader, you try to be as fair as you can.

The situation of the older workers is not much different in the context of the new reforms in the European auto industry. For instance, older workers, who account for 60% of the Peugeot workers, do not have access to "easier" jobs since there is a drastic reduction of management positions and offline jobs. Despite their general fatigue and resignation, older workers in the Peugeot neo-Fordist model still remain attached to the company because of its social life that is personally gratifying (Durand and Hatzfeld, 1999).

An African-American man in his sixties started his career on the Kaizen Motors line at the age of forty-nine, after twenty-five years of service in the army. Shawn is the oldest person in the entire shop, and has been the oldest in all the groups that he joined since he started to work at Kaizen, including the oldest person at the hiring tests. He never felt discriminated against because of his age and felt that he was given equal chances like everybody at Kaizen Motors. His military training helped him to be in a good physical and mental shape. A team leader now, Shawn is grateful for all the opportunities that he had at the Kaizen plant. He feels that it is a great honor and accomplishment for him to keep up with the younger workers in his team.

Another worker in his fifties has a touching story of fairness and inclusion. Three years ago Mason was involved in a motorcycle accident that left him with a blind eye and a skull fractured in multiple places. Despite the fact that he was seriously incapacitated by this personal accident outside of work, the Kaizen family welcomed him back and tried to accommodate his special needs. After four months on medical leave, Kaizen sent Mason to a work conditioning program to get him physically in shape to work again. This was because his muscles "got flabby" on restriction. Another major readjustment for this worker was that he had to learn how to do his job again and to adjust his body to get the best vision with his only eye. He was only restricted from driving equipment in the plant, but other than that, he considered himself very fortunate and grateful that Kaizen allowed him to come back on the line and to readjust to the pace of the line with no push or rush. This example contradicts the rumors that Kaizen will find any excuse to get rid of its older or injured workers.

Some first-shift workers said that they deliberately slow down when they are on the line in order to make their bodies last longer. Most of the team members had the chance to temporarily replace colleagues from the opposite shift, and they noticed the different subculture of work on the first- and second-shift. Arney compares the two shifts:

> On night shift, we run, run, run as fast as you can and go home. On first shift, you are going to be here anyway; the line is running; there's no point in hurting yourself; you cannot make the line run faster.

Although older workers have to live with this incertitude every day when they come to work, they still pray that their bodies last longer because they want to continue getting high wages and benefits at Kaizen. Many of them wish they could quit when their bodies are still strong, but said that they do not know how to cut back or to maintain the same lifestyle without having a job at Kaizen. The sons and daughters of team members are also happy to work at the plant over the summer as seasonal workers because they use the money to pay their college tuition.

Team leaders are patient with the recently hired older workers who are slow learners but want to be "superstars" from the first day (i.e., they want to prove themselves). Team leaders are particularly sensitive to the situation of older workers, calling them "the new wave of diversity that we are going to see in the workforce in the next ten years," a sign that the diversity training increased awareness on the aging of society. According to the team leaders, older workers sometimes even in their late forties or early fifties, who decide to start a career on the line at Kaizen, have the same chances as everybody else. In some instances, team leaders feel that middle age persons perform better on the line because they have previous work experience and a stronger work ethic than "an 18-year old who never paid a bill." In one of the teams, two older temps in their fifties were trained by a permanent team member who was 25-year old, but who worked for five years at the plant.

Experiences of Younger Workers in Teams

The general perception of the workers we interviewed at Kaizen Motors is that an average worker can work continuously in production for twenty years only if he or she starts very young (e.g., at the age of twenty) and moves to leadership positions or easier areas. However, the line makes sure that only the fittest youngsters survive in the long run. This is despite the well-known fact that the turnover rate of workers during their first months on the line is very high. The perception of older workers is that there are 20-25-year olds "dropping like flies," "who cannot do the work" and "whose bodies break down just as much."

At Mazda, workers showed early signs of aging like small lines of fatigue gathered around the eyes and mouths that made them look old beyond their years. Their total wellness programs were intended to bring the physical age down to the chronological age through fitness and other programs, but they were not well-attended (Fucini and Fucini, 1990). At the Kaizen plant, first-shift workers in their mid-thirties called themselves "older workers" whereas second-shift workers as early as their thirties perceived themselves as being "older workers" showing how old age is socially constructed depending on the context and nature of work.

The experiences of younger workers who start their jobs at the plant are similar in the beginning with the experiences of temps. Actually the youngest workers on the line are usually the temps who are typically in their early twenties, whereas the youngest permanent team members are in their mid-twenties. Many of them are drawn to the plant by the generous benefits and compensation, and worry less about their safety. However, the newcomers experience a cultural as well as a physical shock when they start working at the plant as they soon lose weight and also acquire aches and pains in their shoulders, back, neck, and hands. The newcomers are quiet and reserved for awhile until they get the acceptance of their group or "the good-to-go" stamp as they call it.

Occasionally, people who cannot participate in the temporary program are hired off-the-street, but there is a three-to-five-year waiting period from the date of the application. Applicants on this long waiting list can call in and get updates about where they are in line. A young female worker considered herself very fortunate because she was one of the twenty-five workers selected from a pool of 4,800 applications. The hiring tests lasted six to nine months. She had to pass three tests at every a couple of months each. The first test was computerized and included questions on attendance, people's attitudes, and memory. The second test was the actual interview where she was asked how she handles different situations like dating and work ethic. The third test is the physical ability test. Shirley, a recently hired 23-year old, describes the initiation phase for newcomers:

> It was kind of scary because I knew how the temps are going to react knowing that I was hired off the street, but temps were nicer than the team members. Everybody who comes here is given a rough way to go. I probably had one easier because my husband worked here, and people knew who I was. I saw two guys who came here two weeks ago. . . . They were giving [new workers] a rough time, teasing [them] on job performance. "He is never going to make it", they said. I feel really sorry for them. Guys get picked on more than the girls. Come on, you have to give them a chance! It's only their second week!

Teamwork gives younger workers the chance to see for themselves the challenges of growing older on the line. They can learn a lot from the experiences of older workers, especially how to preserve and to protect their bodies. Job enlargement is one of the anti-aging strategies that some of the younger workers use to slow the deterioration of their bodies. They learned the extra jobs on their own time and went to the second-shift to train in order not to leave a hole in their teams. These workers can now not only rotate to the jobs in their teams, but also throughout their whole group. This self-imposed job enlargement not only protected their bodies from getting hurt, but it also alleviated the boredom of the line, as the younger workers could engage in conversation with and gain perspectives from more members of the large group.

The Kaizen Motors plant recently announced a pilot program to recruit high school graduates in order to offset the attrition losses of its aging workforce. This new hiring strategy seems a good idea because only an early start at the plant can ensure that workers are able to fulfill their twenty years of service for the company before retirement. An early start in this career could also help workers start a second career after they retire from Kaizen Motors, whereas now it is very difficult for workers in their mid-fifties to find good jobs.

However, Kaizen workers do not think that targeting high school graduates will work for their plant because high school students do not have the work ethic, dedication, and maturity needed to be a good Kaizen worker. Older workers feel that the ideal Kaizen worker should be in their late twenties or early thirties, have some post-secondary education, and have previous work experience, preferably in manufacturing that will help them appreciate the opportunities that Kaizen Motors has to offer. David is very vocal in expressing his opinion about such programs:

Hiring straight off high school is nuts. You should have a degree when you come in here. I don't like them going after kids because they will be enchanted by the money. Younger are motivated by the monetary rewards, older by the long-term benefits. Older are better workers because they take pride in their work.

On the other hand, the younger workers believe that hiring older workers is also a risky strategy because older workers are more susceptible to injuries. The ideal worker is in the perception of the Kaizen workers, "not too young, not too old." Tanner, a younger worker, comments:

They should try to hire young people, not to hire people in their fifties. I think that's just like asking for an injury. Eighteen is kind of young, I am not sure they are prepared for a career. A lot of people here are for the long-term, whereas 18-year olds do not know what do with their life yet. They might quit after 6 months. The quality goes down but also safety. A 20-year old is not serious enough to work for such a company. He might be asking for a serious accident. At least give them two to three years out of high-school till they get their feet under them.

Contributions of younger and older workers to the teams

The interviews show that the major contributions that older workers bring to their teams are work ethics, stability, wisdom, experiences, patience, dependability, and reliability (excellent attendance, which is extremely important). They make the best trainers and have more thought through and better ideas, especially about safety and quality. However, some of the negative comments about the older workers are that they are more set in their ways, and are slow learners. But team leaders confirm that once they are trained, older workers become good workers. Other perceptions about the older workers are that they complain more and are less satisfied with their jobs.

The major contributions that younger workers bring to their teams are energy, speed, new ideas, enthusiasm and excitement, vitality and creativity, willingness to learn, better eye-hand coordination, better dexterity, willingness to work harder and faster, more physical strength, more technological savvy, and more interest in productivity, change and progress. Younger workers not only bring fresh ideas and perspectives to the team, but also energy and enthusiasm that awaken the teams. Their "gung-ho" attitude, their upbeat tempo, their jokes and humor, uplifts the spirit of teams. The vitality and excitement that young workers bring to work are fundamental aspects of the life on the second shift for instance where workers tend to feel drained, tired and dragging after 10:00 PM. Humor becomes again a central aspect in the environment of teams. Brian, one of the younger workers, thinks that comedy is his unique contribution to the team:

In my team, I like to be silly. This is my gift to the group. I think this is very important, more important than making any car. I bring life, kid around and joke. I try to keep things upbeat; try to make them feel better. They love it!

Older workers are preferred in teams due to their technical superiority (the ability to make a hard job easier) and social skills (their maturity and wisdom leads to less conflicts in teams.) The older workers are also good disseminators of knowledge to teams. Sean, a 39-year old worker, portrays the older workers as learning facilitators and pacifiers of teams:

> It is good to have older workers to work with the younger workers. It seasons them if you want. It helps them become more cured. I would work with older team members because they are more forgiving if you make a mistake. They are more apt to coach and to work with you, to help you learn. They are not in a hurry, you do not feel rushed. Even if we have a *takt* time, it's not a rushed, hurry atmosphere. The younger are more apt to make fun of you, to criticize you, to throw you under the bus than to try to help you work through a process.

The overall preference is for mixed teams that include an equal number of younger and older workers. David's preference for mixed teams is embraced by the majority of workers that we interviewed:

> Honestly you need all of the age groups, including the ones that are close to retiring. They are doing a fantastic job too. If you start with the really young, you will have a lot of inexperienced workers. When I came here, I was young and eager, tremendous speed, I could work forever. The older might not be so fast in endurance, but they have so much experience. The older guy on our team is very proficient. He is not the fastest, but he is the most level-headed. The younger are more argumentative. . . . The young think that they are not getting hurt. The older bring the knowledge, the skills, the younger the get-go, the spunk, the willingness to perform great. We shouldn't lose that, so they can pass it to the young people. We are losing a lot of knowledge after they will retire; you cannot totally replace them. There are so many things they learned after the years.

Suggestions. The majority of team members in both shifts agreed that the older workers make more significant suggestions in their team problem-solving. Team members' perception is that although younger workers put out more ideas, the older workers bring better ideas. The older workers bring valuable experience to the table from their previous workplaces, as well as have more experience with the lean system of production. They understand more fully the logic of lean systems and the overall assembly of a car, whereas the younger workers are more intimidated by the whole production process at the beginning. Older workers are more concerned about finding different ways to make their jobs easier because they know that they are there for the long run. However, they are not very open to the suggestions that come from their younger colleagues. Younger workers consider that older workers as being rather set in their ways and resistant to change. Only the risks of getting hurt stimulate the older workers to search for better ways of accomplishing their jobs.

Productivity. Fifty percent of the team members interviewed find that younger workers are more productive, whereas fifty percent find that the productivity of younger and older workers is the same, otherwise older workers would lose their jobs.

Quality. The overwhelming majority of team members from both shifts confirmed that the older workers are more quality conscious, because they have more experience and have adopted the lean mentality (e.g. "Older people are more experienced. They tell the new people: "this is right, this is wrong."). A few team members believed that although older workers are more experienced with quality control, they have a laissez-faire attitude when it comes to defects. Aston complains:

> The older workers do not care much. They cannot be pushed as easily as the younger. Younger will do what they are asked to do in terms of quality. They are more obedient. It's a lot of wear and tear on my body over ten years. There's no incentive here to go above and beyond. I have seen people here making defects every day and they still get the same kind of money. The older workers are more concerned of their jobs, and if something is wrong, they will not necessarily tell a supervisor and hope that inspection will not catch up. You have to respect yourself and set up higher standards.

Safety. The overwhelming majority of interviews showed that the older workers are the most safety-conscious workers in teams. They are concerned with their personal safety because a lifetime of work on the line leads to injuries, aches, and pains that cumulate throughout their bodies (e.g. "We are realistic that we will not last forever. The young don't understand the long-term effects of injuries."). Older workers are equally concerned about the safety of their colleagues (e.g., a friendly pat on the shoulder when somebody is exposing himself to danger) and the safety of customers. Mackey argues:

> Even if somebody will yell at me for stopping the line, that's fine. I will not let a car go out the door that will hurt anybody. People could get killed if you don't do something right. You have to remember that we have to do this right.

Gung-ho or Guru: Relations between the Younger and Older Workers

The younger workers are often called the "gung-ho" workers of the line. Although the expression sounds Japanese, it is in fact a Chinese word representing the communist industrial cooperatives where workers work together with a "spirit of teamwork, courage, and wholehearted dedication" (*Random House Dictionary*, 1998). Adopted by the military, the expression is now used with a slightly derogatory and ironical connotation that shadows the meaning of teamwork and emphasizes an "offensively ardent, overly zealous, and perfervid" attitude (*Random House Dictionary*, 1998).

Kaizen Motors' gung-ho workers have a superman mentality and a macho attitude toward work. They are eager to move up and prove themselves by putting out 150%. The gung-ho workers pair nicely with the gurus of the line, the older workers, who think twice before they act, have a larger vision of their work, are interested in the well-being of others, not only in productivity, and avoid futile movements and activities.

Brian, a 36-year old second-shift worker, is an overzealous gung-ho. He loves his job a lot and is very excited by the numerous opportunities for promotion and professional development. Consequently, he takes advantage of all the opportunities that he has: he knows thirteen jobs instead of five. Although the second shift ends at 2:30 AM, he stays at work till 5:00 AM every day to participate in five different quality circles. Brian says that he feels tired in the morning, but that he still wants to challenge his brain, not only his hands and legs. One of his quality circles got him the Platinum medal and a $200 prize, and now his circle is shooting for the $1,000 prize and the trip to Japan.

The older workers take the roles of Gurus or spiritual masters of the teams. Gurus want to do their jobs better and smarter rather than harder and quicker. For the Gurus, safety comes first, if it is their personal safety or the safety of their team members, quality second, and productivity, third, which is in line with the Kaizen values and philosophy of production. Gurus are leaving their gung-ho attitude aside after their long tenure at the Kaizen plant takes a toll on their bodies. From their role of spiritual masters of the teams, the older workers pass on advice that encourages safer behavior to their younger colleagues. Gary notices:

> The older bring a little bit more experience. They will say: "Hey, this is going to hurt you in about a year. You need to stop doing it. Slow down! You have all the life to do it!" They do not have the "go-getter" attitude.

Along the same lines, Henry, an older team member comments:

> The older are smarter. They go around the block. The younger work the hardest way. The older will tell them: "What are you doing? There's an easier way to accomplish this." The experience steps in.

Morgan, also an older team member, elaborates:

> The younger guys are more ambitious and love their job a little bit more. They want to try harder for awhile. After awhile, it fades away. The younger try harder for the company, which pushed the older (workers). The older have more knowledge. When you are younger, you don't think that it is going to hurt you eventually. You say: "I can do it, I can do it!" Whereas when you are older, you say: "I can do it, but it can hurt me eventually." You are a better thinker as you get older.

Although the connection between teamwork and family has been a constant pattern throughout the study, the older workers tried to avoid taking the mother or the father figure in teams. They are not threatening or judgmental, and in most cases, pass advice only if they are asked. The gung-ho workers might have a go-getter attitude, but they are more inconsistent in their work and also in their personal relationships with the other workers: they tend to "blow up" when they have conflicts with other team members or to have a "melt down" when they mess up three to five cars in a row, and people jam up trying to help them.

The gung-ho and the guru are actually symbols of distinct generalized others. The gung-ho is the "young other," whereas guru is the "old other." These generalized others provide for the individual's unity of self (Mead, 1964: 154). Team member's use of these meaningful labels show each worker's ability to gain the perspective of the different other, which is so vital in the successful functioning of diverse teams.

Younger workers bring a fresh approach to work that helps the older workers feel younger. Younger and older workers sometimes socialize with each other outside of work, as in one instance one of the favorite pastimes for an Kaizen worker was to play golf with another team member, who was fifteen years younger. Humor distinguishes itself again as the most fundamental dimension of interactions between younger and older workers. There is a certain teasing going on between team members: newcomers are ridden to keep up the pace in the beginning, and then after they get comfortable with the pace of the line, they cut back in the same manner: "Hey, grandpa, keep up! Hurry up, old man!" The older workers do not get offended, and even joke about themselves in an attempt to prevent further ridicule. This type of diversity-driven joking is a vital sources of entertainment on the line.

Conclusion on Age at Kaizen Motors

Of the theories considered here, team intensification theory works the best. While the Kaizen teams are rather homogenous in terms of age, they brought young and old workers together on successfully functioning teams. The young respected the older workers and vice versa. They became communities of fate where young and old team members would work together. Usually first shift workers have even fewer conflicts with each other than second-shift workers because they are more mature and learned each other's hot buttons. Generally team members prefer to work in mixed teams with a balanced number of young and old workers. This is because the different skills in teams complement each other with younger and older workers being good at different things.

But team intensification theory was implemented less well between the shifts. There were more conflicts reported between first-shift workers and second-shift workers during their temporary assignments in the opposite shifts. A first-shift worker reports that second shift workers are quicker to report them than to help.

Second, the integration and learning perspective worked with age since the older workers did bring something special—the wisdom that comes with experience. The very term guru speaks of this special knowledge, and to some extent, the strength and endurance of the younger workers is something that they brought to the workplace. However, when older workers retire—after having been unanimously recognized as the teams' champions of safety, quality, and problem-solving—teams will lose valuable knowledge and expertise.

Third, Kanter's theory on tokenism and team intensification theory have fewer chances of operating since the two shifts are homogenous in age, but very different from each other. The complaints against the workers from the opposite shift exist particularly because the younger and the older workers do not have that many chances of getting in contact, and therefore they maintain prejudices against each other.

Older workers made two important recommendations to Kaizen Motors, and most of them revolve around the issues of safety. First, the older workers insisted that Kaizen should not outsource the easy jobs or transfer them to temps because the older workers can prolong their careers only if they have access to easier jobs. The following interview with Alex presents the dire situation of some older workers:

> Cross-docks, fork drivers, and stuff like that, most of the easy jobs should not be eliminated. They should not hire temps to drive the forklift or trucks. Those were the jobs that the older people were planning on having, so we do not have to work that much. They are eliminating all these easier jobs for lower pay. We do not have a lot to look forward. When we were hired, we were promised . . . that these easy jobs will be ours. I am here middle-aged and I don't see where I can work in twelve years. The company says that this is the way companies are doing now, that we have to cut costs.

The second most important suggestion is related to the fitness and well-being programs. Older workers would like the company to encourage more stretching exercises. If the company would compensate workers for the time spent in the gym, this would be seen as a safety investment, and ultimately as an investment in their workforce.

In conclusion, as the older workers continue to be the teams' champions on safety, quality and problem-solving, Japanese transplants should reconsider the role of older workers in the whole context of lean production. Old age and lean production should not be considered a misfit. On the contrary, older workers should be accommodated in such a way that both employers and employees would be able to take advantage of a mutual beneficial employment relationship.

Chapter 7

THE UNDERDOGS: TEMPORARY WORKERS AND TEAM DEGRADATION

> I don't like my team leader, but I respect him. He did not train me. He is just jumping all over me. Team members ask me: "Why does he talk to you like this?" "Because I am a temp, that's why. I can't say nothin." *A temp*

> It was hard to get up to speed. There was a guy in particular who rode me a lot: "You suck!" he told me. He probably thought that this is joking, but he was also chiding me a little bit to work faster and harder. *A temp*

> If I could, I would hire them on the spot. I would like to see all temps be full-time members.... Temps come and go. The stability of your team is always in question. I would rather work with people that I know and see everyday. *A team member*

While the previous chapters analyzed three types of visible diversity (gender, race and age), this chapter explores the largely invisible impact of diversity on teamwork–being a temp or permanent worker. This analysis includes the experiences of temporary workers in teams, their contributions and fit within the teams, their emotions, and their identity transformations during their stay at Kaizen Motors. The unequal status of temporary workers is discussed in the context of teams, as well as the experiences of female and older temps.

The early participation observation studies of Japanese transplants in California, Michigan, Kentucky, Indiana, England, and Canada provide a detailed account on the nature and dynamics of teamwork at Japanese transplants. But these Japanese transplants had very few temporary workers, save those who were sent over from Japan for start-up purposes. Since then, Japanese transplants have added temporary worker programs and used them as their main form of hiring. Now, temporary workers are up to a quarter to a third of their total labor force.

Temporary workers have an impact as an artificial type of diversity on team dynamics, and ultimately, on team performance. But it is a form of employment inequality rather than a visible form of diversity. This chapter analyzes the impact of temporary work on the dynamics of production teams and is the only study that we know of that examines the effects of temp work in the auto industry, particularly at one of the top Japanese auto makers in the US.[1] Clearly, the use of temporary workers creates a great divide in the life of teams and an unmistakable duplicity in the employment relationship in the context of high performance work organizations.

Temporary Workers: The Duplicity of an Employment Relationship

Temporary employment is considered "one of the most spectacular and important events that have occurred in labor markets recently" (Nollen, 1996). However, the US has one of the lowest shares of temporary employment among the OECD countries with less than 5% in comparison with 32% in Spain and other countries (OECD, 2002). The demographics of this form of employment in the US shows that 53% of temporary help agency workers are women, and 50% of temps are under the age of 35 years old. However, the number of black and Hispanic temps is nearly double the number of black and Hispanic workers in full-time jobs (US Department of Commerce, 2005). Temporary workers tend to have less job satisfaction, be less educated, and have higher turnover (several hundred percent) than the permanent workers (OECD, 2002). On average 60% of the female temps and 80% of the male temps choose this form of employment for economic reasons: namely, their inability to find regular full-time jobs. But they hope that temporary work will lead to permanent employment (Kalleberg et al., 1997). Most of the temp jobs that women have are secretaries and data entry positions, and only 5% of all the female temps and 8% of the male temps are assembly-line workers (Kalleberg et al., 1997).

There are strategic and cost advantages to hiring temporary workers. First, the use of temporary workers increases flexibility to meet market demands during downturns and helps reallocate resources toward other strategic areas such as sales and marketing. Second, temps reduce costs. They may cut wage costs in half, most often eliminate pension benefits, drastically reduce health insurance costs, and shift many human resource department costs (e.g., testing potential workers) to an outside agency. The most important disadvantages of using temps are smaller than the advantages but nonetheless significant. First, they create inefficiencies because temps usually have fewer specific jobs skills since they are new, and they need to be trained. They also create a two-tier workforce that increases problems with corporate loyalty, confidential information, smooth teamwork, and corporate identity and culture. The use of temps also reduces the pool of candidates for management positions (Nollen and Axel, 1996). One society-wide advantage of temporary employment is that it helps some disadvantaged workers (young, women, minorities, and unemployed) to develop more skills and to strengthen their human capital (Nollen, 1996).[2]

Most of the temps have experienced unstable, entry-level jobs that lack opportunities of involvement, training, and trust. Temporary work leads to a fragmentation of workforce because temps themselves are dissociated from one another (Smith, 1998). This especially happens when temps start competing with each other to impress management (Smith, 1998). Temps also dissociate from one another as they do not want to branded with the image of being "bad temps" (lazy, uncommitted, and with poor work ethics). Although temp work appears to open opportunities for re-skilling, it in fact deepens social inequality and offers less mobility opportunities for both full-time and temporary workers (Smith, 1998).

Temps can fill a hole and help a team when a team member is injured, but the can also create a great divide in teams. Temporary work arrangements affect the power dynamics between employees and employers (Kalleberg et al., 2000). Work in blended teams with permanent and temporary employees undermines the loyalty of standard employees as the past research shows that managers delegate the tasks of socializing, training, and supervising temporary workers to permanent employees (Geary, 1992; Pearce, 1993; Smith, 1994). Thus, the core employees end up having increased responsibility, decreased mobility, and lower promotion opportunities (Davis-Blake et al., 2003). Temporary workers can be used sometimes as a disciplining factor for the standard employees who understand that they can be replaced at any time with temps if they limit their efforts or if they have union sympathies (Davis-Blake and Uzzi, 1993; Smith, 1997).

The coexistence of a two-tier workforce with the rhetoric of inclusiveness, equity, and respect for people is a good example of the contradictory logic of these new forms of organization (Smith, 2001). The high performance work systems that are participative systems by definition ironically do not share the intellectual and social rewards with the temps who contribute to their organization's success. The use of temp work creates big morale problems or dilemmas in teams, as "the foundations of temporary employment—transience, detachment, and disposability—threaten the building blocks of participative work cultures" (Smith, 2001).

Temps at Kaizen Motors were asked to describe their experiences of working in their current team, as well as compare their experience with other teams they worked with at the plant. Permanent team members were asked to talk about the advantages and disadvantages of working with temps on a team. Similarly, they were asked to recall their own experiences as temps before being hired as permanent workers at the Kaizen plant. Therefore, the following data include stories from temps from their first days and up to five years at the plant.

Kaizen Motors uses temps for three main reasons: fluctuations in business volume, replacing team members on leave (manpower), and developing a better hiring pool (recruitment) (Kaizen Motors, meetings in 2006). Temporary workers in lean systems are a buffering strategy to fill-in for sick or injured production workers, but they also protect the regular production workers from being fired during times of recession. Thus, temporary workers become indispensable actors of lean production.

Temps account for 11% of the total workforce at the Kaizen plant, which are roughly 20% of the total of assembly-line workers, and 58% of the temps work on the second-shift, while 42% of them are on the first-shift (Kaizen Motors Administrative Records, 2006). The yearly temp turnover rate was 44%. Most of the temps had previous manufacturing experience and decided to join the temporary program as a strategy of getting in permanently at the Kaizen plant. Others had only fast-food experience or worked previously in dead-end jobs.

Following the post-9/11 economic recession, Kaizen Motors had a hiring freeze that resulted in a waiting time of more than five years for temps to get a permanent position. Due to the hostile reactions of workers and the community, the company recently decided that temps should not work at the plant for more than twenty-two months before they are let go, and that they should be hired (if they are to be hired) in eighteen months. However, the survival of the fittest principle of the line guarantees that only the most qualified and fittest temps last two years, meaning that only 10% to 15% of temps will be offered permanent employment in the end. Temps are evaluated every six months. The most important indicators of their performance are attendance and quality, but the team leader also writes a report/ recommendation about their attitude and work ethics.

Temp Experiences on the Line

Temps can easily be recognized at the plant as they wear T-shirts or hats with the name of their temp agency and usually have new hardhats. These distinctive symbols are used to help easily identify the temps on the line in case they need back up. Temps make on average $400 a week (with overtime) and usually loose between fifteen to forty pounds during their first six months on the line. Many temps drive four hours (two hours back and forth) every day to get to the plant because working at Kaizen is considered an excellent job opportunity.

Temps have a cultural shock during their first days at Kaizen Motors. The first contact with the immensity of the plant and the nature of work on the line is overwhelming and intimidating. The turnover rate of temps is 44.4%, which leads to a constant flow of incoming and outgoing newcomers in teams. Some of them do not come back from their first lunch at the plant, but most quit during their first two weeks. Production is particularly affected when temps walk out during their assignments, as the line will be understaffed that day (Parker, 1994). From the beginning, this process of self-selection removes those workers who are not fit for the job.

The past literature on temps shows that temps have to go through many critical personal hurdles like identity crises, stigma, uncertainty, alienation, and low status and prestige (Rogers, 2001). They also have to contend with difficulties in the organization (e.g., role ambiguity, constant surveillance, performance pressures, initiation rituals, and constant transfers), and the ensuing difficulties at home due to low wages, sub-standard health insurance, and job insecurity. According to one worker, even simple things like buying a house can be difficult—"who is going to give a loan to a temp?" Temps end up either being overworked in high-status and high-paying jobs, or underworked in low-status, low-paying jobs (Kalleberg, 2007). Overworking in the context of high performance work systems means overtime and work intensification. As a result, these workers are exposed to stress and other health problems that affect workers' well-being (heart problems, diabetes, depression, and immune system deficiencies) (Kalleberg, 2007).

Fairness and the lack of distributive justice

The general consensus of both temps and full-time members is that the short-term temps deliver lower quality in the beginning until they learn the whole process, whereas the long-term temps (after six months) are held at a higher quality standard than the full-time members. Team members agree that temps are more easily fired for quality issues although the full-time members sometimes deliver even worse quality. Team leaders yell at temps, pick on them, and write them up easier than the regular team members. Temps are under constant surveillance and are held at higher standards because there is the assumption that temps will restrain their output once they get hired. At the same time, the firing process of full-time members is lengthy and complicated, so management is trying to control the employees hired from the very beginning, so that they will be the cream of the crop.

The double standard goes further when it comes to compensation and benefits. Temps are officially employees of the temp agencies and make half of what the full-time members make for the same work. They do not receive the typically large bonuses twice a year, and their health insurance is much thinner than the insurance offered to Kaizen Motors team members. Also, temps cannot participate in the Kaizen Motors award ceremonies or get discounted tickets (although some of the team members will buy these tickets for them).

Only a few temps admitted that team members give them a hard time, such as looking down and talking trash to them. When all the employees received MP3 players for the company's anniversary, a few of the full-time members complained that temps got this symbolic bonus. Some team members can be very cruel and offend temps by telling right in their face that they are "nothing but a temp!" Team leaders may also lose their patience and yell more at them. However, most of the full time members treat temps well after they end their trial period of six months.

Emotions in the Face of Instability and Insecurity

Emotional labor is a significant component of temporary work as temps try to be as friendly, helpful, enthusiastic, and nice as possible to ensure that they get permanent employment or other important assignments (Rogers, 2001).

Most of the temps are content with the opportunities that they have at the plant. They all remember the thrill and excitement they had when they received the temporary hiring letter, which gave them clear expectations and specified that the duration of employment is for two years.

Emotions are intertwined with the perceptions of fairness in teams. Attachments between team members are combined with reciprocal feelings of animosity. Temps sometimes have feelings of animosity towards the full-time members because they receive considerably more benefits while they are held at lower standards. On the other hand, a few full-time members feel animosity towards temps because temps take over places in the first shift, while some of the permanent workers are stuck on the second shift.

These double standards and feelings of instability and insecurity build up mixed emotions for both temps and full-time team members. Full-time members tend to distance themselves from temps because they do not know how long temps will last on the line. This cold reception makes each temp's transition into the work group even more difficult. Al, a current temp and former union organizer at a supplier plant, is bitter about the condition of temps on the plant:

> Oh, yeah, I've seen people crying. I've cried many times, but I try to hold my mouth. I've seen people curse, throwing things. We can get in a lot more trouble than a team member. They can walk us out. I've seen people going crazy. They go nuts. A temp is on probation for six months for arguing so badly with his team leader. He was very professional, but you could see his eyes steaming.

In some cases, team members did not speak with the new temps on their teams for a month. After awhile, full-time members start opening up more towards temps. When temps are transferred to other teams, both temps and team members are saddened by the move. It's a brain drain, as well as an emotional drain, as they get attached to each other and have to cut the ties again. Vince, a 22-year old temp, describes his experience as a line traveler:

> You have to watch what you say. Some people are religious, some like to do dirty talk. You learn that when you jump from group to group. I don't like to move because you get attached to people. They will just tell you that next morning you are going to work with another group because they are short on people. I hate to move again.

Temps are on an emotional roller-coaster during their stay at Kaizen Motors. In the beginning, they are quiet, reserved, and fighting for group acceptance. Then, they tend to be vulnerable and moody as they see that they are the underclass of the line. After two years, many of them become aggravated and frustrated as time is running out. Team leaders do not see the real personalities of temps until they are hired permanently mostly because team members teach temps to keep their thoughts and ideas to themselves. The symbolic interactionist perspective frames the covert behavior of temps as the dramaturgy of teams, where temps manage their performances with masked identities on front-stage, while having a more critical back-stage manner (Goffman, 1959)

Full-time members sometimes associated temps with "slave labor, "exploitation," "alienation," and "outcasts." They were more angry and vocal about the situation of temps on the plant, whereas only two out of the thirteen temps complained about their situation during the interviews. Most of the temps showed an overt enthusiasm for their jobs at Kaizen Motors. Was this a fake enthusiasm, or is it that temps are indeed very excited about their new job opportunities at the plant? They probably did not want to show their discontent for fear that a research study might end the temp program, but also because their enthusiasm had already become a part of their persona at work. As Smith (1998) has shown, most of the temps' criticisms about their company revolve around their frustration about being permanently hired. And they have cause for worry since only 10% to 15% of temps become permanent employees.

Past research explains that many temps enthusiastically show their commitment for their new jobs which are perceived as great opportunities for personal development. Temps also develop new employment identities as they proudly associate themselves with the high status and prestige of their temporary employers. Temps develop enthusiasm for their jobs as a form of resistance to the alienation of their work, their selves, and from others (Rogers, 2001) or because of their low employment trajectories (Smith, 1998). To the extreme, some temps said that they would even work as temps forever for top companies (Smith, 1998).

Similarly, Kaizen Motors' permanent workers who had to temp between three and five years (the grandfather group) were not bitter at all when they look back at the time they spent as temps. Even when they became discouraged for waiting for so long, they realized that their job has better benefits and more opportunities for professional development than any of their previous employers. Ernest, who was a coal miner, drove 113 miles back and forth for five years as a temp until he was given a permanent position at the plant. He is grateful for the job he had as a temp (an easier work than in the coal mine) and "couldn't have wished for more." All of the temps assure us that if Kaizen Motors will offer them a permanent position tomorrow, they will take it in a heartbeat.

Thus, the precarious employment situation of temps is not generally associated with negative emotions (stigma, embarrassment, shame, fear), but also with the central emotions of enthusiasm and gratitude. Although some of the temps we interviewed may have managed their impressions of enthusiasm, our interviews with permanent workers and former workers about their temp experiences confirm their overall viewpoint toward Kaizen Motors. The proof is that once they are hired permanently, or after they leave the company, they do not recall their previous experiences as temps in overly negative terms. Many of them said "I wish I had come here earlier," proving that their overall experience at Kaizen Motors is a largely rewarding experience. However, temps who worked for years and were not hired on as permanent workers have positive feelings toward most team members but express considerable negativity toward the company.[3]

Female and Older temps

Kelly Girl is the prototypical image of the female temp—"brisk, efficient and unthreatening"—because "she is just a temp" (Henson, 1998). Although most of the female temps hired by the Kelly Services are still doing clerical and office work, some of them trade in the Kelly Girl image for a Rosie the Riveter career in automotive assembly at Kaizen Motors.

But temps are exposed to abusive situations (Rogers, 2001), and female and older temps are even more vulnerable because of their precarious status. Marianne, a female temp, describes her emotions and fears:

> I was so afraid that they will not be giving me a chance if I do not keep up, but I was given a chance. It was a very good experience. I was the first temp they ever had in that group. They said: "If we do something wrong, we are sorry. Please tell us because we never had a temp." I remember in one occasion that a man, who was derogatory about every temp, told to my face that the only reason I was here as a temp was to find a good husband who makes good money as a team member. I told him: "Don't worry, it will not be you! I don't want to share my money with you either."

Sandra comments further about her difficulties:

> First month, I was very uncomfortable because they did not talk to me. I was miserable. I hear now my colleagues wondering if a temp will make it or not. I wondered if they said that about me. It is harder for women temps. They automatically judge a woman. They make bets on women, if they will make it or not.

Thus, the drama of teams includes a back-stage and a front-stage (Goffman, 1959). As much as team members try to be inclusive with the temps, their difference stands out and their performance is judged behind the scenes. The temporary status seems to be the most divisive type of "otherness" on the line. In the beginning, temps carry with them the stigma of the marginal worker. Although an invisible dimension of diversity, this employment status creates a greater divide in teams than any of the other visible dimensions of diversity like gender, age, and race. One female temp advises other temps who start working at Kaizen Motors that temp agencies instill a fear of being fired before they go to the plant, so they will work hard. However, she discounts this fear because the firing process is lengthy, and if temps make mistakes, they are given many chances to improve.

Because of equal employment opportunity legislation, the company does not impose any age restrictions on temps so forty five to 50-year old temps have the same chances of getting hired on permanently as 20-year old workers. Justin, a 45-year old temp in his first month at Kaizen, is amazed at the opportunities that he is offered:

> Kaizen is doing a superb job. They treat temps the same. If you are a temp or

old, there is no difference. If they see you struggling, everybody will bend their back to help you. This is the best place I ever worked. I wish I came earlier.

Team leaders show an enormous amount of respect for the middle-aged workers who join the temp program. Their stand is that older temps have the same chances like all the other temps, no better or worse. However, they confess that it takes a little bit more time and patience to train the older temps because they are more set up on their ways and more nervous. They also try to work faster so they can prove themselves.

Temps' Contributions to Teams

Suggestions and Problem-Solving. Temps experience conflicting demands when it comes to suggestions. On one hand, team members appreciate that they bring fresh perspectives to the team, but on the other hand, temps as newcomers to a group are rather reluctant to voice their opinions. Willie says:

> They do not want to speak, they do not want to stand out, they want to fit in and blend as easily as they can. I did not see any temp standing out and suggesting something. They do not want to sound silly, they do not want to make the team mad, because they can suggest something that nobody wants to do. So they just blend in. They can suggest, but they won't because they would be afraid to rock the boat. If they make someone mad, then they will lose more than they would gain.

Most of the temps confessed that they do not feel ready to offer any suggestions about a job they know so little about. Some of them said that they will suggest more after they finish their training and learning. Other teams have democratic voting and if the temp made a good suggestion and has unanimous support, then the suggestion is adopted by the whole team. In other teams, if temps have an idea, they will ask one of the team members to present it to the group. When a temp had a good suggestion in a *kaizen* project, the team did all the paperwork, and the temp did not get credit because the temp was technically not a Kaizen Motors employee. These situations speak volumes about the feelings of insecurity and fear that temps experience until they gain the full acceptance of the group. Also, Kanter (1977b) would say that temps are trapped in their roles and cannot expand their responsibilities to things outside the boundaries of their status.

Productivity and Quality. Temps have on average a lower productivity because of their lack of experience. Only the promise of permanent employment makes them overachieve and have higher productivity (see the Hewlett-Packard case in Nollen and Axel, 1996: 183). Regular team members label temps either as overachievers, if they do well, or as slackers, if they do poorly, but seldom as average workers. Even when temps manage to have an equal performance with the full-time team members, it is visible to everyone that they try a lot harder.

These extreme performance labels demonstrate Kanter's (1977b) concepts of the "exaggeration of differences" and "performance pressures" that temps face due to their token status (Kanter, 1977b). Anderson, a permanent team member, describes the performance of temporary workers as follows:

> When they come in, they are trying to overachieve and do as hard as they can. Temps will do whatever you want them to do. The temp that I know always works extra because he needs a good recommendation from the team leader and group leader. Temps are so on top of it. They make sure everything is done perfect. Temps will clean the floor with a toothbrush and will do it as fast as they can. Then, our team leaders will say: "Look, a temp can do it, then you can do it!" Yes, you can do it for a day or two but not for ten or more years.

The image of temps as overachievers can also be explained by the fact that permanent members expect the worst from temps and are very pleasantly surprised when they do a good job (Parker, 1994). Temps overachieve also as a form of resistance to structural disadvantage and to the stigma of marginal worker (Smith 2001). The overachieving temp is associated in the literature with the image of Sisyphus, who no matter how much he struggles, his efforts are underappreciated and has to start everyday all over again (McAllister, 1998).

Safety. The temps' biggest challenge is safety, which is the top priority for everybody at Kaizen Motors. But temps are particularly torn between their desire to succeed under pressures to perform well, and their own risk of getting hurt. Wayne, a team member, describes their situation:

> Full-time members are more concerned with safety. Temps will try to prove themselves. Go-go-go, and that's when you can make more mistakes or hurt yourself. They will get injured. And if they are injured, they will not be hired. Temps do not feel comfortable to say "this is something that hurts me" because it will be a ticket to straight out of the door. If I were a temp, I wouldn't say anything. I would keep my mouth shut, work my 24 months, get hired and then I will say: "This hurts."

Kaizen Motors has officially announced that injury on the job is not an impediment for the permanent hiring of temps. This change of policy was needed because temps tended to hide their injuries for fear that they are going to be denied permanent employment. Kaizen allowed injured temps to return to their positions on the line according to one temp's experiences. However, most of temps show distrust towards the new policy change. After the change, team leaders only found that a small number of temps (i.e., 5% to10%) slowed down or were hurt all of a sudden after they were brought on as permanent employees.

Temps and Team Dynamics

Some teams were not composed of regular members for as much as four years because they always had a team member on medical leave. This caused the team dynamics to be constantly changing as there were always new temporary workers who needed to be trained. One of the group leaders noticed that when a new person joins a group, it takes the group back to what they called the "forming and storming phase."

Temps mean manpower to work groups. The main advantage of using temps is that it gives more flexibility to the team in the job rotation cycle and helps filling in when team members are absent. The first day after the July shutdown, manpower was terrible: people were on restriction, on vacation, involved in car crashes or called on duty in the military. This is when temps were brought in to keep the line going. Temps are human buffers who help teams to control unpredictable environments. It is safe to say that teams would not be able to function and accomplish all the jobs in the rotation cycle if they did not have temps. Paradoxically, these peripheral workers become a vital, core category of workers who keep the line running. Temps are a disadvantaged category of workers who work with less benefits, pay, prestige, and status for the welfare of teams, and ultimately for the welfare of the lean systems. Ironically, the security of teams is based on the insecurity of temps.

The most important keyword that constantly comes up in these interviews is the metaphor of team as a family, where temps are the adopted or step-children. Most of the temps are adopted by their new team families like one of their own and participate in all the activities, including eating lunch together. Angelo, a team leader, compares the process of training a temp with the process of educating a child. "Training a temp is like raising a kid: If you let them cut corners, they will be disrespectful. If you start them off with good habits, they will have good habits."

In other teams, temps are reminded of their different status and are told that they should participate in team activities only if they want to (an example of exaggeration of differences, Kanter 1977b). Many teams require temps to prove themselves over one to two months to see if they are going to make it. So temps have to go through a transitional process in taking extra steps to show their desire to blend in and fit into the team, and only then will the group come forward and embrace them. In the end, there are teams that practice either minor or lengthy rituals of acceptance for newcomers that are common in highly cohesive groups in organizations (Gabriel et al., 2005). Keith, a new temp, describes his job-related initiation process:

> They were a little hard on me in the first weeks. I came from a desk job. I never worked in a factory before, and I was not physically fit. It was hard to get up to speed. It was a guy in particular who rode me a lot: "You suck!" he told me. He probably thought that this is joking, but he was also chiding me a little bit to

work faster and harder.

Jack, another temp, shares a slightly different perspective:

> I heard horror stories, but it never happened to me. Before I came here, people
> told me that the temps are treated badly here, but I never experienced it. First
> days, people helped me and treated me good. They hazed me a little bit, but not
> too bad: "You will not make it in two weeks!" or "Are you sure are you coming
> back from lunch?"

Other teams take advantage of the inferior status of temps and give them the
hardest jobs in the job rotation cycle, on the grounds that "temps are fresh" and
can do the tougher jobs whereas the veterans of the line have been already injured on those jobs. Temps do not have any choice but to accept those jobs
without complaint. Kayla, a female temp, explains that "this is the nature of the
beast: to always look down at people beneath them." The democratic participation in teams is under question when temps are seen as insiders and outsiders at
the same time (Smith, 2001)

Some team members developed solidarity with the temps and backed their
demand to be hired in less than twenty-two months. Team members insist that
temps should be hired between six to twelve months. According to the survival
of the fittest principle, bad temps are going to eliminate themselves during their
first year, and after that, there is only a waiting game that increases the anxiety
of temps. They also say that if temps are considered part of the team, they
should be allowed to participate in the reward ceremonies and share other company benefits such as discounted tickets. Team members also wanted the company to be more transparent about the temps hiring process, and they recommended that the company regularly meet with temps and give them statistics
about how many temps are hired every month and when each new cohort of
temps might be hired.

The situation of temps on the plant is ambiguous as they are insiders and
outsiders at the same time. Some teams treat temps as their own members, others have a waiting game restraining their involvement until the temps successfully pass the first six months. Many full-time team members embraced a sympathetic but still critical position toward the temps. Bruce, a team member,
elaborates:

> Temp workers are by and large in the worst situation than anybody in all this
> plant. They can't say: "You guys are hurting me, I can't do this." They are out
> of here, if they do it. To me that's slave labor. It is very much out of character
> for our company, but it's profitable. If you ask me, this was a much better plant
> before the temps came in. In the beginning, they used temps only on pick vaca-
> tion times, that was a good time for everybody, then they realized that they can
> use temps for cheap labor. It's a no-win situation for everybody except for the
> company. I understand that companies are doing it, but not companies that are
> as successful as Kaizen. You have to go to temporary workforce when times
> are hard, but when times are great, you have to take care of the people that got

you there!

When temps have a successful transition from the short-term to long-term status, they earn the full support and encouragement of the full-time members. Some team leaders ask their temps to wear regular T-shirts and hats after they've been with their teams for more than six months, as a sign that temps have become one of their own.

Permanent members are sympathetic to them because they had to go through the same difficult times in their "teen" years on the line. They not only give temps' emotional support, but also advocate for them on human-resources-related issues. Austin, a current temp, describes his odyssey of being hired:

> I am honest, horrible at interviews. They asked me what I do not like about the job. I told them that I do not like repetition, and I flipped the interview. I was about to lose my job. I will not kiss up to them. My colleagues and my team leader called HR and the higher-ups to tell everybody that I am a good worker. I am a hard worker, but if you do not say what they want you to say, they will not hire you.

Temps work with six to seven different groups till they are permanently hired. This experience is a diversity lesson in itself. As they soon come to realize, they are not treated the same by the different groups they join. In some groups, they might have to face the perception that temps should pick up team members' slack, whereas other teams can organize baby-showers or even parties for them when they get hired on. Temps are socialized differently from shift to shift, which leads to tensions in their teams. Second-shift teams felt that they have to retrain the temps who came from the first shift (the older shift) and taught them the proper way.

The immersion of temps into teams highlights the duplicity of their employment relationship with middle management. Team leaders are in charge of the training, coordination, and safety of temps, but this is an ambiguous relationship. While temps are subordinates of the team leaders in the plant, they are not even Kaizen employees because their official managers are at the temporary work agencies. Smith (2001) gives many examples from the high-tech industry where managers tries to correct the inequality of the system by including temps in minor social functions, giving them paid days off, providing modest cash rewards, and even recommending them for the permanent employment interviews. But team leaders cannot erase the temp's "temporary reality."

The leading disadvantages of working with temps in a team are their low retention rates and the sometimes poor quality of their work (at least in the initial phase). Temps are initially trained to do two jobs that usually are the easiest in the job rotation cycles. Therefore, if a team member is on restriction and has to be replaced with a temp, the rest of the team will rotate only three or four instead of five jobs. Consequently, the permanent workers have to rotate the most difficult jobs more often, which takes a toll on their bodies in the long run and exposes them to more injuries. Temps also hurt and ache because of the repetitive movements of doing only two jobs over and over again.

Temps are the double-edged sword as they hurt and help the stability of teams at the same time. They come in handy when the team is short on manpower. Teams invest time and energy into training them, but they can always be moved to other teams. The circulation of temps is a cycle of frustration for teams. When the full-time team members come back from restrictions, temps will be "borrowed" by other teams or groups. Erica, a permanent team member, describes the main disadvantage of working with temps:

> They do not stick around for very long. They are moved to other groups and you lose all that training. We lose six weeks of training them for nothing. We don't get any reward out of it. To the company is a big advantage, but it costs us.

In a company obsessed with quality, the many defects that temps turn out is a major disadvantage. Team members give a number of reasons why temps deliver such a poor quality work in the beginning: (1) they do not receive the best training because trainers expect that half of them will leave soon; (2) their training often only lasts a week to a month if they are needed on the line; (3) the screening of temps is handled by temporary employment agencies and is not at all rigorous, and (4) the physical adjustment to assembly-line work often eliminates workers rather quickly (feeding back into item 1 above).

The exaggeration of differences associated with their token status (Kanter, 1977b) can easily transform temps into team scapegoats. If team members are tired and hurt, they blame the temps for having the easiest jobs, which temps often take because they are not skilled enough to do the more difficult jobs. If temporary positions open up in the day shift, the permanent workers on the second shift complain that temps are taking spots on the first shift that permanent workers would have gotten. Most of all, team members get aggravated when temps are transferred to other teams and replaced with new or inexperienced temps. Many full-time team members do not like to train new temps when they have already trained numerous others.

Most of the permanent team members are bitter-sweet regarding the impact that temps have on their teams. They built up frustrations against them, while at the same time they are sympathetic about their situation. Richard, a regular team member, sheds some light on this dichotomous perspective:

> The bad part is that they are doing the same thing we are doing for half the money. They get hurt and most of them have to mask it until they get hired, and then they are getting an operation. We know about it, but we are not going to tell anybody. It happens all the time. It's not fair for them to work here two years before they are hired. I don't need two years to see you are a good worker. They learn the easiest jobs, and we end up doing the hardest jobs twice or third a day. On a long run, people are getting hurt.

The overwhelming majority of team members mentioned that if they could choose, they would definitely prefer to work with full-time members instead of temporary workers. Full-time members are preferred to temps because they know all the jobs in the job rotation cycle and are not overstressing the other team members. At the same time, some workers say that they prefer to work with temps because they are hard-working and complain less than full-time members, especially less than the disgruntled workers from the first shift with long tenure at the plant.

The interviews showed that team members are ambiguous about the purpose or use of temps on the line. However, none of the team members believed that the use of temps protects their jobs. An extreme position is taken by one worker who believes that the company is conspiring to use more temps:

> You should have enough people to build a car. I don't think they use the temps because they want to avoid lay-offs, but because they do not want to hire people. We do not have anything on paper saying that they will not have lay-offs. They would like to have a factory full of temps, trust me! They will make much more money.

Conclusion on Temps

Despite the team rhetoric of horizontal integration, the use of temporary workers creates a schism in teams, which leads to conflict because of the social stratification of the line. Teamwork can increase the power imbalance between team members with temps becoming the underclass of the assembly line. Temporary employment generates confusing work relationships. Temporary workers can be viewed as a commodity whose main purpose is not necessarily to deliver good work, but to be disposable (Vosko, 2000). As he puts it, the use of temporary workforce delivers flexibility to employers and "precariousness" to temps. Temps are subjected to more work intensification and higher demands than the permanent workers as well being subject to alienation, marginalization, and resistance from many permanent workers who consider them to be overachievers (Vosko, 2000). They fit many of the characteristics of Kanter's theory (1977b) such as role encapsulation, exaggeration of differences, and scapegoating. Similar conclusions with less of a commodification view can be reached from equity and distributive justice theories that stress the workers' reactions to unequal rewards for the same work (Adams, 1965; Cropanzano et al., 1997; Roemer, 1996). All in all, the existence of temps and their unequal treatment are violations of both team intensification theory and the core principles of *Toyotism* that require that workers be treated equally. Kaizen Motors pays a higher price for temps than they realize.

The interviews reveal that temporary workers are not a unified, holistic category of workers. Team members consider that the experiences and contributions of temps to teamwork vary depending on the length of their service with the company. Consequently, the interviews showed that temporary workers form two distinct classes: short-term temps (with a job experience of less than six months) and long-term temps (with a job experience of 6 months and up). Short-term temps, the underclass of the line, struggle with their jobs in the beginning and their quality suffers, whereas the long-term temps, the lower class of workers, who usually work for the company up to two years have a performance equal and sometimes better than regular team members.

This study shows that Kaizen temps do not experience technical marginalization (i.e., they are not assigned to the most physical or dirtiest jobs). However, despite some team efforts to treat temps as their own, many temps feel social marginalization because of the duplicity of their employment relationship. Temps have an enthusiastic attitude toward work that shows that they borrow from the prestige and status of their adopted company while trying to internalize the positive organizational culture and participatory philosophy. This study shows an even deeper fragmentation of the temp workforce than previously anticipated with both short-term and long-term temps.

Chapter 8

CONCLUSION

As one of the first studies on diversity in the mature phase of lean production, this study reveals the nature of interactions between co-workers in mature teams and how diversity affects the group and team functioning in the lean systems. As American society grows more diverse, there is a tendency not to question if the increasing diversity has a positive impact on the performance of teams. This study uses team intensification theory to show the context, conditions, and circumstances in which "diversity works better," as well as the few instances in which it does not.

Women, African-Americans, and Older Workers

This study contributes in many ways to the literature on Japanese transplants as well as team diversity. First of all, the Kaizen study analyzes the dynamics and interactions of Japanese style production teams in detail. Our study of Kaizen Motors shows how mature teams with experienced team members evolved in the context of mature lean production. We enrich the literature on Japanese transplants with unique chapters on temporary and older workers—the only account that we know of regarding the role and experiences of temporary workers and older workers in high performance work organizations in the auto industry. Each of these chapters shows that diversity in teams is experienced in different ways.

Women, despite their minority status, are more enthusiastic and satisfied with their overall work experience at Kaizen Motors. The empowerment, weight loss, high wages, and respect that they enjoy at work leads to almost an identity transformation. Despite their preoccupation with quality and safety, we do not have a clear indication of how the presence of women influences the key performance indicators of each group. However, their presence in teams is desired mainly because of their attention to quality and the talk and chat that they bring to the line, which alleviates team members' boredom. Consequently, women are important contributors to the team climate and spirit (an intermediate variable) that indirectly leads to higher performance. The most surprising finding of this chapter is that good teamwork leads to interpersonal relationships and affairs between team members, conducive to a high rate of divorce in the long run. This is a disadvantage of teamwork not previously mentioned in the literature on teams.

Race relations in this Japanese transplant are more difficult to access. The presumed colorblind attitude of teams is a consequence of the longevity of teams. Racial minorities, particularly African-Americans, reveal more overt enthusiasm and satisfaction with their jobs at Kaizen, which strengthens our criticism of Kanter's theory of tokenism. African-Americans are in the Kanter danger zone, but they have received promotions, and most are working well within the system. There is much evidence that they are distinctly proud of being in a system that works so well and produces cars that the American public wants. Some white team members describe humor and joking as the most central aspect of the racial interactions in teams. They have a positive influence on the team climate, as joking is one of the most desirable activities on the line. However, the analysis raised some uncomfortable issues about white privilege concerning minority promotions and "I-never-met-a-Black-person-until-I-came-to-Kaizen-Motors" syndrome.

Older workers have an interesting pattern of interaction in teams with the young workers. Many younger workers have a "gung-ho" attitude, while the older workers take on the role of "gurus," or spiritual masters of the teams, passing on advice mainly on quality and safety. After a lifetime of working on the line, just-in-time production takes a toll on older workers' bodies, and they see themselves in the situation of not having many "easier jobs" to choose from. Older workers are considered the teams' champions of problem-solving, quality and safety, and their retirement is going to be a great loss for their teams, and ultimately, for the company.

Unlike gender, race and age, temporary workers are the most problematic aspect of diversity at Kaizen Motors even though this category is not generally regarded as part of the American response to diversity. Despite many being younger, temporary workers actually represent a wide range of ages as they contract with an external hiring firm separate from Kaizen Motors. Being temporary means accepting a peripheral status when working with team members, who are core workers. Temps face both ambiguity and duplicity in this work situation, and the teams themselves face a major internal division. The fragmentation of temps is much deeper than previously anticipated, with short-term temps being excluded from inclusion in teams, whereas the long-term temps are treated as regular team members. Temporary workers are held to higher standards than the regular members and have the tendency to hide their injuries. Ironically, the stability of teams is built upon the precarious employment status of the temps.

Kaizen Motors uses temporary employment to buffer the regular team member from the ups and downs of economic production. In the process, management also threatens participative teams and reminds regular team members that they can be easily replaced (Smith, 1998). As a result, temporary work introduces many negative outcomes.

Theoretical Contributions

This study of Kaizen Motors introduces team intensification theory to explain four factors about work on the line: (1) the process of creating workable diversity among high performance teams, (2) the stresses of the system in eliminating workers who cannot handle the pressure, (3) the unexpected impacts on families as team intensification goes beyond the job into workers' personal lives, and (4) how workable teams can be denigrated by not following the tenets of team intensification theory. First, team intensification theory explains how diversity works rather well at Kaizen Motors by getting team members together and focused on common tasks. Team members work together on interrelated tasks and achieve a result that is recognized throughout the industry and among customers around the world. A clear group identity is formed around teams and groups through a powerful generalized other. Team intensification theory takes a number of elements from the revised contact hypothesis but places this theory in a team intensive context that the theory does not generally encounter (Allport, 1954; Pettigrew and Tropp, 2006). It presented the optimal conditions that lead teams to an attitude of gender- and color-blindness. Team members came to appreciate each other's differences and how this could contribute to a better team.[1] Contact with different people in a team setting brought out many of the emotional satisfactions that diversity can bring. For women it seemed to be the marital or family advice that a different perspective could bring to men on an assembly line. For African-Americans, it was more of the humor and different ways of viewing life that white men might learn on the job. Both women and African-Americans brought spice and variety to what amounts to a rather boring and high pressure job. When this is coupled with contact in a team that is a community of fate (nearly at total institution in Goffmanian terms) with each team member being equal, and where success is a predominant outcome, the conditions for the revised contact hypothesis are largely met (Besser, 1996). In fact, the team nature of lean production provides nearly perfect conditions for the revised contact hypothesis much better than more limited teams or individualized production.

Symbolic interactionist theory was used to develop multiple identities with multiple generalized others that each of them may have developed. The major question for the success of lean production is the social construction of the 'team' as the primary generalized other. And to some degree, this also lessened the remaining generalized others outside of work. The concept of generalized other is the bridge that links the theory of symbolic interactionism to the question of difference and diversity.

Second, many workers quit their jobs at Kaizen Motors because the work was too hard on their minds and bodies, the job required mandatory overtime often crowding out time for family and community activities, and a number of other reasons. Working at Kaizen was hard, especially for women and some men, but no one promised potential employees a rose garden. Some women were particularly concerned about how the corporation handled pregnancy and injuries. So team intense work filtered out workers from the beginning.

Third, there were a number of positive and negative outcomes from team intensification that were probably not anticipated by proponents of lean production. On the negative side, the intensity of teams led to men and women working together for long periods of time when mandatory overtime is a constant feature of the job. This led to a number of romances, and an impression by Kaizen workers that their divorce rate was rather high. Some of these workers, who met on the job and dated, ended up getting married to each other. Thus, the contact may have been too extensive for some marriages to survive, and this has consequences for many of the children who might be involved. On the positive side, some women developed positive identities, which we referred to as superwoman, which led to feelings of confidence, attractiveness, and standing in the community that they would not have otherwise gained. Women lost weight, had more disposable income than ever before, and used this income to become more attractive in a number of ways. Men lost weight too, but the identity change was not as dramatic. African-Americans who did well in the plant were promoted to team leader and group leader, and would often express their pride at doing the job right. This filtered out into their communities. Thus, the long arm of this particularly intense job reached out into families and communities for better or worse.

Fourth, team intensification theory shows how teams can be diminished by not treating workers equally and introducing systematic inequality with temporary workers. Temps were paid less, had fewer benefits, and had the obvious difficulty of job insecurity. They were switched around more and officially they were not even Kaizen employees (they technically were employed by the temporary help agencies). The temporary worker situation not only brought dissention into the team environment, but it also led to the breakdown of the team concept itself. Temps were largely ignored by teams, and when they were part of the work group, this neglect was a loss. Temps were kept in a state of constant hopefulness of being hired on full-time. Some were hired, but many of them had their hopes dashed. Temps threatened regular workers by being an obvious pool of workers who could take their jobs, and the temps often worked harder and were prone to take almost any task.

While team intensification theory explains the important points of what we set out to cover, other theories of diversity in teams had limitations. This does not mean that they are not good theories, but their fit with this particular context of lean production was problematic. Ely and Thomas' (2001) integration and learning perspective had only a partial effect. Women did bring a more quality- and safety-oriented approach to teams, but there was no specifically female or

African-American approach to assembling automobiles. Ely and Thomas' primary example of a research office that sought to obtain social research grants about minorities is a far cry from an automotive assembly plant. However, the integration and learning perspective did apply somewhat to age where the 'gurus' did have specific automobile and assembly-related skills, especially tied into safety, that they could transfer to the younger 'gung-ho' workers. Consequently, the integration and learning perspective was somewhat limited with learning or gaining insight on production-related skills.

Although Kanter's theory about the token presence of minorities creating undue observation and attention to errors may have worked in an earlier period of this plant and at other plants that clearly had sexual and racial harassment, there is not much to support it at Kaizen Motors. Despite minority status, women, racial minorities, and even temps report higher satisfaction and enthusiasm than the majority workers, which partially contradicts Kanter's theory on tokenism (Kanter, 1977b). The numerical representation of tokens in our sample (one member out of five team members, 20%) does not perfectly fit the proportions used by Kanter in her theory (15%). Further, zero diversity and high diversity teams do not function at their best as women and sometimes racial minorities tend to develop frequent conflicts among themselves. However, moderate to low diversity teams have a more pleasant and enjoyable experience on the line, and minorities in these teams show surprisingly high levels of satisfaction and pride in their work. The one situation in which Kanter did apply was to the temporary workers who did suffer early role encapsulation and exaggeration of differences. In sum, we do not claim that this study disproves either theory, but rather note that the circumstances of automotive production do not seem to mesh well with these two theories when compared to team intensification theory.

Recommendations

One of the most surprising findings on the topic of gender is that teamwork provides an emotional source of support that helps some families, but also undermines others. Emotional support can be a doubled-edged sword. At the same time, both male and female auto workers try to balance difficult work schedules, including shift work and overtime that erode their relationships at home in the long run. According to both the qualitative and quantitative data used in the study, balancing work and family is the greatest source of dissatisfaction at Kaizen Motors. Therefore, work-family programs should be the central part of the inclusion and gender diversity policies at Japanese transplants. Balancing age between day and night shifts would reduce the possibilities of dating. One single mother went further recommending that Kaizen Motors open a private school for the company employees, similarly to the daycare facility. The advantage of this rather costly initiative would be that school schedules could be adjusted according to the parents' working schedules, while children could be raised in the culture of teamwork and learning to appreciate other cultures and civilizations. This kind of initiative would strengthen the community of fate at the Kaizen Motors, while creating a pool of future workers that are inspired by the teamwork principles from an early age.

Kaizen Motors is regarded by its workers as one of the most diverse companies for which they have ever worked. The minority groups (Asian, African-American and Hispanic) are surprisingly more satisfied and appreciate their jobs at Kaizen somewhat more than the white workers. Racial and ethnic diversity leads to a more enjoyable and fun experience at work, which is a fundamental dimension of the life on the line. However, some assembly-line workers seem to misunderstand and misinterpret the principles of affirmative action, equal employment and diversity at work. From their perspectives, diversity means "meeting the quotas" of minorities (fairness perspective), and they do not see the connection with the business objective. Comments about "working hard to meet the quotas of blacks" can be offensive for the minority workers, therefore the company should have a clear, straightforward message on "why diversity is good" and what the advantages of diversity in teams are on the shop floor. Kaizen Motors and other similar Japanese transplants should do concerted efforts to offer more diversity training to assembly line workers, not only to management. And finally, an African-American worker recommended the company promote more minority singers at the reward ceremonies as a sign that their cultural heritage is valued and promoted.

Concerning the age factor, the company should prepare the transition and the transfer of knowledge from the older workers (primarily in shift one) to the younger workers (primarily in shift two). According to the team leaders, the mother company practices shift rotation in Japan, and these practices have been adopted by some of the Kaizen transplants in US where workers have to rotate the shifts every two to three weeks. If the company provides incentives for the older workers to move to the second shift, this new policy would have a positive effect on work-family programs. While the company ensures that the knowledge accumulated in almost twenty years of assembly line experience is not lost, younger team members have the chance to learn easier ways of doing their jobs from the older workers. Since the major complaint of workers at the plant is the poor balance between work and family life, such a policy would allow more second-shift workers to transfer to the first shift, which indirectly would help them spend more time with their young families and children. This policy contributes to a more thorough inclusion of women at the plant since most of the second-shift women are single mothers with small children, while first-shift workers mostly have adult children.

Another potential positive effect of balancing teams by age is reduced probability of dating, based on the presumption that most of the dating or extramarital affairs in teams usually happen between members of the same age cohort. This new policy would indirectly combat a major disruption in the life of teams that leads to an alarming rate of divorce. However, some of the potential negative effects of this policy are that the older workers will be unhappy and bitter to move to second shift. Some of the oldest workers have always worked first shift only because they had the luck to be hired in the initial phase of the plant. This policy would support the spirit of the community of fate at Kaizen Motors, giving the older workers more advisory roles (Gurus) in the second shift, while strengthening the families affected by the tempo of lean production. Also, based on the assumptions of the contact hypothesis, this age-balancing of teams would reduce the prevalence of conflicts between shifts.

Temps—Central or Peripheral to the Drama of Lean Production?

Ultimately, the company will have to clearly define the role of temporary workers, or temps will continue to simultaneously be the pain and panacea for teams in the indefinite future. This means that Japanese auto makers would need to address a central issue that contradicts their inclusion rhetoric. Since temporary employment as well as high performance work systems are on the rise, these companies should draw on more effective strategies concerning the inclusion of temps and try to clarify the role of temps in the context of their workforce. First, by targeting temps with previous manufacturing experience or auto experience, temps could become equal actors on the participative systems arenas. Second, companies should be aware of the inequalities generated by this employment relationship and should try to hire more permanent workers and fewer temps. Third, if temps are acknowledged as central to lean production and the company's mission by being temporary, they should be given higher compensation than team members (not drastically lower wages and benefits) since their working conditions are tougher and job security is so much lower. In the end, the ambiguity of temps is generated by the company's lack of transparency concerning the role that temps fill in lean production. Until they end this ambiguity, the contradictions of this form of "diversity" will continue within their teams and in the public eye.

Appendix 1

INTERVIEWER'S GUIDE

Demographics:
1.   Current Position / Title:
2.   Group number:
3.   Team number:
4.   Gender:
5.   Age:
6.   Race-Ethnicity:
        a. African-American
        b. Caucasian/ White
        c. Hispanic
        d. Asian/ Pacific Islander
        e. Biracial
        f. Other
7.   Employment Status:
        Full-Time or Part-Time Team Member
        Temporary Worker
        Other
8.   Highest Level of Education:
        College
        Some College / Technical School
        High School / GED
        Other
9.   How many years have you worked for Kaizen Motors?
10.   How long have you worked with your current team?
11.   Did you work in a similar field before? If yes, what type of job did you do?
12.   Do you participate on a Quality Circle or in the Suggestion System? Why or
        why not?

Teamwork:
13. What do you like the most about your team? What do you like the least about your
     team?
14. Think about the best worker on your team (it can be you) and tell me what makes her/
     him to be the best?
15..Tell me how the team leader and the group leader influence how you work in a team.
16. If you could choose, would you work in a team or individually in the future? Why?

Gender interactions in teams:
17. How do men and women get along in your team?
18. What are the advantages and disadvantages of working with men/ women in a team?
19. What do men and women bring to the team?
> Who is more active with suggestions and solutions to problems?
> Who is more productive?
> Who is more concerned with quality?
> Who is more concerned with safety in your team?

20. If you could choose, would you prefer to work with more women or more men in
team? Why?

Women only:
21. What is it like to be a woman and to do this kind of work?
22. What unique contributions do you think you add to the team as a woman? Do the
other team members listen to what you have to say? Do your co-workers value you as a
member of the team?
23. Can you give any suggestions that will help your organization to include the contributions of women/ men more fully?
24. As a female working in this industry, do you have any specific concerns or issues that
you would like to share with us?

Age interactions in teams: (Younger is under 40, and older is 40 and over)
25. How do younger and older workers get along in your team?
26. What are the advantages and disadvantages of working with younger/ older workers?
27. What do the younger or the older workers bring to the team?
> Who is more active with suggestions and solutions to problems?
> Who is more productive?
> Who is more concerned with quality?
> Who is more concerned with safety in your team?

28. If you could choose, would you prefer to work with younger or older workers in your
team?
29. What is it like to be a younger / older person and to do this kind of work?
30. What unique contributions do you think you add to the team as a younger/ older person? Do the other team members listen to what you have to say? Do your co-workers
value you as a member of the team?
31. Can you give me any suggestions or ideas that will help your organization to include
the contributions of young/old workers more fully?

Employment Status (Temporary and Permanent Workers):
32. How do temporary workers and full-time team members get along in your team?
33. What are the advantages and disadvantages of working with temporary workers / full-

time Kaizen Motors team members?
34. What do the temporary workers or full-time team members bring to the team?
>   Who is more active with suggestions and solutions to problems?
>   Who is more productive?
>   Who is more concerned with quality?
>   Who is more concerned with safety in your team?
36. If you could choose, would you prefer to work with more temporary workers or more full-time Kaizen team members in your team?

Temporary workers only:
37. How is it to be a temporary worker and to do this kind of work?
38. What unique contributions do you think you add to the team as a temporary worker?
>   Do the other team members listen to what you have to say?
>   Do your co-workers value you as a member of the team?
39 Can you give me any suggestions or ideas that will help an organization to include the contributions of temporary workers more fully?

Race and Ethnicity:
40. How do the workers of different races and ethnicities get along in your team?
41. What are the advantages and disadvantages of working with people of different races and ethnicities in your team?
42. What do the workers of different races and ethnicities bring to the team? Think about suggestions and solutions to problems, productivity, quality and safety.
43. If you could choose, would you prefer to work with workers of the same race or people of different races and ethnicities in your team?

For minority workers only:
44. How is it to be a minority worker and to work with this team?
45. What unique contribution do you think you add to the team as a minority worker (e.g. African-American, Hispanic)?
>   Do the other team members listen to what you have to say?
>   Do your co-workers value you as a member of the team?
46. Can you give me any suggestions or ideas that will help your organization to include the contributions of minority workers more fully?

Conclusion:
47. If you could choose your co-workers, what would your ideal team look like in terms of composition?

Appendix 2

METHODOLOGY AND DATA COLLECTION

The degree of diversity in groups was measured as low (0 to less than 25%), moderate (25% to less than 50%), and high (greater than 50%). The percentage of group diversity was measured by numbers of white females (WF), minority males (MM), and minority females multiplied by two because it contains two aspects of diversity. The sum of these three numbers was then multiplied by 100 and divided by the total number of members in the group (TG). The result is the following formula for group diversity (GD):

$$GD = \frac{(WF + MM + 2 \times MF) \times 100}{TG}$$

The generalized other was measured in terms of how workers evaluate themselves and their team members. Key words such as 'they,' 'the team,' etc. will be used to determine how the generalized other is framed.

Sampling and Study Population

The study included only team members working on the assembly-line (production workers). Women and minorities were not excluded from the study; on the contrary, this study benefited from the feedback of female and minority team members to document the competitive advantage of diverse work teams. Sampling is the process of selecting individuals for a study in such a way that descriptions of those elements accurately portray the characteristics of the total population from which the elements are selected. Purposeful sampling was used in order to select informants that will best answer to our research questions. In order to select a theoretical sample, the following five stages were performed.

Stage 1: Sampling by department. Since the focus of this project is production teams, we selected initially only the production departments. Thus, we narrowed down the search to six production departments in assembly, paint, plastics, stamping and power train. One particular assembly department seemed to be ideal for many reasons. First, this department is the site where all the body parts are assembled together and come together as a finished product. Work in this department is typical assembly line work. Further, some of the other departments could not handle the work disruptions caused by the project. This assembly unit also had almost the same demographic representation as the plant (3.1% minority females, 16.8% white females, 9.5% minority males and 70.7% white males).

Stage 2: Sampling by type of work: This assembly unit has a total workforce of roughly 1,000 employees. From this sampling frame, we eliminated maintenance and other off-line personnel from our pool, and we came up with a total of 32 groups (about 700 team members) that work directly on the line. Our sampling unit is the work group, because we did not have centralized data and demographic information available for teams.

Stage 3: Sampling by group size: Work groups in Assembly 1 vary largely in size from the minimum of 14 members to the maximum of 28 members. Therefore, we narrowed down our pool one more time in order to include only groups of a standard size of twenty members (with two members more or less).

Stage 4: Sampling by degree of diversity: The degree of diversity in groups was measured as follows: (1) low was 0 to less than 25% diversity, (2) moderate was 25% but less than 50%, and (3) high diversity was greater than 50%. The percentage of group diversity was measured by numbers of white females (WF), minority males (MM), and minority females multiplied by 2 because it contains two aspects of diversity. The sum of these three numbers was then multiplied by 100 and divided by the total number of members in the group (TG). The result is the formula mentioned in the first paragraph of this appendix.

Stage 5: Sampling by shift: After selecting groups by degree of diversity, there was only one low, one medium and one high diversity group from each shift. The diversity groups are categories on two shifts with the labels: low 1, medium 1, high 1, and low 2, medium 2 and high 2.

Stage 6: Final sample: This sample of 115 workers represents 16.5% from the total workforce of the approximately 700 assembly-line workers of the Assembly unit (see table A2.1).

Table A2.1: Final sample (Total is 115 workers)

Diversity Group	White females	Minority males	Minority females	Total Points	Total TM	Percent Diversity
First Shift						
Low 1	2			2	15	13%
Medium 1	4	2	1(x2)	8	18	44%
High 1	7	2	2(x2)	13	21	62%
Second Shift						
Low 2		2		2	19	11%
Medium 2	4	1		5	20	25%
High 2	7	4		11	22	50%

The six diversity groups were composed of sixteen teams (three teams with zero diversity, five teams with low diversity, four teams with medium diversity, and four teams with high diversity). Only 87 workers from the initial sample of 115 workers participated in the study. Some of the workers were on restriction, in their summer vacation, extended weekend, military duties, maternity leave, funeral leave etc. The last two white male teams (ten members) were excluded from the sample because we reached theoretical saturation, a point where data started to become repetitive. The sample included eight out of sixteen teams with zero and low diversity, so it included enough information on homogenous teams.

REFERENCES

Adams, J. S. 1965. "Inequity in Social Exchange." Pp. 276-99 in Leonard Berkowitz (ed.) *Advances in Experimental Social Psychology*. NY: Academic Press.

Adler, Paul, 1992. "The Learning Bureaucracy: New United Motor Manufacturing, Inc," *Research in Organizational Behavior*. 15:111-194.

————.1999. "Teams at NUMMI," pp. 126-150 in Jean-Pierre Durand, Paul Stewart, and Juan José Castillo (eds.). *Teamwork in the Automobile Industry*. London: Macmillan Press.

Albertijn, Michel, Johan Van Buylen and Leen Baisier. 1999. "Teamwork at Opel Antwerp," pp. 346-365 in Jean-Pierre Durand, Paul Stewart and Juan José Castillo (eds.) in *Teamwork in the Automobile Industry*. London: Macmillan Press.

Allport, Gordon. 1954. *The Nature of Prejudice*. Reading, MA: Addison-Wesley.

Aoki, Mashaiko, Gregory Jackson, and Hideaki Miyajima (ed.). 2008. *Corporate Governance in Japan: Institutional Change and Organizational Diversity*. NY: Oxford University Press.

Appelbaum, Eileen, Thomas Bailey, Peter Berg and Arne Kalleberg. 2000. *Manufacturing Advantage: Why High Performance Work Systems Pay Off*. Ithaca: Cornell University Press.

Arrow, Holly, Joseph McGrath and Jennifer Berdahl. 2000. *Small Groups as Complex Systems: Formation, Coordination, Development and Adaptation*, Thousand Oaks, CA: Sage.

Babbie, Earl, 2004. *The Practice of Social Research, Tenth Edition*, Belmont, CA: Wadsworth.

Babson, Steve, 1995. *Lean Work: Empowerment and Exploitation in the Global Auto Industry*, Detroit: Wayne State University Press.

Bacharach, Samuel, Peter Bamberger and Dana Vashdi. 2005. "Diversity and Homophily at Work: Supportive Relations among White and African-American Peers." *Academy of Management Journal* 48(4):619-44.

Barker, James, 1993. Tightening the Iron Cage: Concertive Control in Self-Managing Teams, *Administrative Science Quarterly*. 38:408-37.

Bartunek, Jean. 2003. *Organizational and Educational Change*. Mahwah, NJ: Lawrence Erlbaum.

Batt, Rosemary and Virginia Doellgast. 2005. "Groups, Teams and the Division of Labor" pp. 138-61 in Stephen Ackroyd, Rosemary Batt, Paul Thompson and Pamela Tolbert. *The Oxford Handbook of Work and Organization*. NY: Oxford.

Berggren, Christian. 1993. *Alternatives to Lean Production*. Ithaca, NY: Cornell University Press.

Berk, L. 1989. "Neuroendocrine and Stress Hormone Changes during Mirthful Laughter." *American Journal of Medical Sciences*. 298:390-6.

Besser, Terry, 1996. *Team Toyota: Transplanting the Toyota Culture at the Camry Plant in Georgetown, KY*. Albany, NY: SUNY Press.

Blumer, Herbert. 1969. *Symbolic Interactionism: Perspective and Method*. Englewood Cliffs, NJ: Prentice-Hall.

Bond, Meg. A. 2008. *Workplace Chemistry: Promoting Diversity through Organizational*

Change. Hanover: University of New England Press.

Bonilla-Silva, Eduardo. 2006. *Racism without Racists, Second Edition.* London: Rowman and Littlefield.

Bonilla-Silva, Eduardo, Lewis, Amanda, Embrick, David. 2004. "I Did Not Get That Job Because of a Black Man...." The Story Lines and Testimonies of Color-Blind Racism." *Sociological Forum* 19(4):555-581.

Braverman, Harry, 1974. *Labor and Monopoly Capital,* NY: Monthly Review Press.

Brulin, Göran, and Tommy Nilsson. 1999. "The Swedish Model of Lean Production: The Volvo and Saab Cases," pp. 327-345 in Jean-Pierre Durand, Paul Stewart, and Juan José Castillo (eds.). *Teamwork in the Automobile Industry: Radical Change or Passing Fashion?* London: Macmillan Press.

Burawoy, Michael. 1979. *Manufacturing Consent: Changes in the Labor Process under Monopoly Capitalism.* Chicago: University of Chicago Press.

Business Week. 2005. "Japan: the Downside of Downsizing" *Business Week.* November 7.

Bybee, Roger. 2008. "Whitewashing Honda." *Multinational Monitor.* 29(3):8.

Camuffo, Arnaldo and Stefano Micelli. 1999. "Teamwork and New Forms of Work Organisation in Fiat's 'Integrated Factory'," pp. 218-235 in Jean-Pierre Durand, Paul Stewart, Juan José Castillo (eds.). *Teamwork in the Automobile Industry.* London: Macmillan Press.

Carli, Linda and Alice Eagly. 1999. "Gender Influences on Social Influence and Emergent Leadership", Pp. 203-222 in Gary Powell *Handbook of Gender and Work.* Thousand Oaks, CA: Sage.

Chalice, Robert. 2008. *Improving Healthcare Using Toyota Lean Production Methods, Second Edition.* Milwaukee, WS: ASQ Press.

Charmaz, Kathy. 2006. *Constructing Grounded Theory. A Practical Guide through Qualitative Analysis.* Thousand Oaks, CA: Sage.

Chattopadhyay, Prithviraj. 1999. "Beyond Direct and Symmetrical Effects: The Influence of Demographic Dissimilarity on Organizational Citizenship Behaviour" *Academy of Management Journal,* 42:273-87.

Cohen, Susan. 1993. "New Approaches to Teams and Teamwork" pp. 27-48 in *Organizing for the Future: The New Logic for Managing Complex Organizations.* SF: Jossey-Bass.

Cole, Robert. 1974. *Japanese Blue Collar: The Changing Tradition.* Berkeley: University of California Press.

———. 1980. *Work, Mobility and Participation.* Berkeley: University of California Press.

Collins, Patricia Hill. 2000. "Gender, Black Feminism, and Black Political Economy." *Annals of the American Academy of Political and Social Science,* 568:41–53.

———. 1986. "Learning from the Outsider within: The Sociological Significance of Black Feminist Thought." *Social Problems,* 33(6):S14–S32.

Cooley, Charles Horton. 1998. *On Self and Social Organization.* Chicago: University of Chicago Press.

———. 1964 (1902) *Human Nature and the Social Order.* NY: Schocken.

Cornette, Guy, 1999. "Saturn: Re-engineering the New Industrial Relations," pp. 85-106 in Jean-Pierre Durand, Paul Stewart, and Juan José Castillo (eds.), *Teamwork in the Automobile Industry: Radical Change or Passing Fashion?* London: Macmillan Press.

Cox, Taylor. 2004. Problems with Research by Organizational Scholars on Issues of Race and Ethnicity, *The Journal of Applied Behavioral Science,* 40(2):124-45.

Crenshaw, Kimberley. 1991. "Mapping the Margins: Intersectionality, Identity Politics, and Violence against Women of color" *Stanford Law Review.* 43(6):1241-1299.

Cropanzano, R., J. C. Howes, A. A. Grandey, and P. Toth. 1997. "The Relationship of Organizational Politics and Support to Work Behaviors, Attitudes, and Stress." *Journal of Organizational Behavior.* 18:159-80.

Creswell, John, 1998. *Qualitative Inquiry and Research Design: Choosing among Five Traditions,* Thousand Oaks, CA: Sage.

Davis-Blake, Alison, Joseph Broschak, and Elizabeth George. 2003. "Happy Together? How Using Nonstandard Workers Affects Exit, Voice and Loyalty Among Standard Employees." *Academy of Management Journal,* 46(4):475-85.

Davis-Blake, Alison and Brian Uzzi. 1993. "Determinants of Nonstandard Work: A Study of Temporary Workers and Independent Contractors." *Administrative Science Quarterly* 38:195-223.

De Waal, Cornelius. 2002. *On Mead,* Belmont, CA: Wadsworth/ Thompson Learning.

Delbridge, Rick, 1998. *Life on the Line in Contemporary Manufacturing: The Workplace Experience of Lean Production and the 'Japanese' Model,* Oxford: Oxford University Press.

Denzin, Norman and Yvonna Lincoln. 2000. *Handbook of Qualitative Research,* Thousand Oaks, CA: Sage Press.

———. 1998. *Collecting and Interpreting Qualitative Materials.* Thousand Oaks, CA: Sage.

Dohse, Knuth, Ulrich Jürgens and Thomas Malsch. 1985. "From Fordism to Toyotism: The Social Organization of the Labour Process in the Japanese Automobile Industry." *Politics and Society.* 14:115-46.

Dovidio, John, Peter Glick, and Laurie Rudman. 2005. *On the Nature of Prejudice.* NY: Blackwell.

DuBois, W. E. B. 2005 (1903). *The Souls of Black Folk.* NY: Barnes and Noble Classics.

Durand, Jean-Pierre, Paul Stewart, and Juan José Castillo (eds.), *Teamwork in the Automobile Industry: Radical Change or Passing Fashion?* London: Macmillan Press.

Durand, Jean-Pierre and Nicolas Hatzfeld. 1999. "The Effectiveness of Tradition: Peugot's Sochaux Factory" pp. 173-201 in Jean-Pierre Durand, Paul Stewart and Juan José Castillo (eds.), *Teamwork in the Automobile Industry.* London: Macmillan Press.

Durkheim, Emile, 1984. *The Division of Labor in Society,* NY: Free Press.

Edwards, Richard. 1979. *Contested Terrain: The Transformation of the Workplace in the Twentieth Century,* NY: Basic Books .

Egan, Toby Marshall. 2005. "Creativity in the Context of Team Diversity: Team Leader Perspectives," *Advances in Developing Human Resources,* 7(2):207-25.

Ely, Robin, 1994. "The Effects of Organizational Demographics and Social Identity on Professional Women," *Administrative Science Quarterly,* 39(2):203-36.

———. 1995. "The Power in Demography: Women's Social Constructions of Gender Identity at Work," *Academy of Management Journal,* 38(3):589-646.

Ely, Robin, Thomas, David, 2001. "Cultural Diversity at Work: The Effects of Diversity Perspectives on Work Group Processes and Outcomes," *Administrative Science Quarterly,* 46:229-73.

Evans, Randy, and Walter Davis. 2005. "High Performance Work Systems and Organizational Performance: The Mediating Role of Internal Social Structure," *Journal of Management,* 31(5):758-75.

Ezzamel, Mahmoud, and Hugh Willmot. 1998. "Accounting for Teamwork: A Critical Study of Group-Based Systems of Organizational Control," *Administrative Science*

Quarterly, 43: 358-6.

Freyssenet, Michel. 1999. "Transformations in the Teamwork at Renault," Pp. 202-217 in Jean-Pierre Durand, Paul Steward, and Juan José Castillo (eds.) *Teamwork in the Automobile Industry*. London: Macmillan Press.

Fucini, Joseph, and Suzy Fucini. 1995. *Working for the Japanese: Inside Mazda's American Auto Plant*, NY: Free Press.

Gabriel, Yiannis, Stephen Fineman, and David Sims. 2005. *Organizing and Organizations: An Introduction , Third edition*, Thousand Oaks, CA: Sage.

Gaertner, Samuel, J. Mann, John Dovidio, A. Murrell and M. Pomare. 1990. "How Does Cooperation Reduce Intergroup Bias?" *Journal of Personality and Social Psychology*. 49:692-704.

Gaertner, Samuel, M. Rust, John Dovidio, B. Bahman and P. Anastasio. 1994. "The Contact Hypothesis: The Role of a Common In-group Identity on Reducing Intergroup Bias" *Small Group Research*. 25:224-29.

Gaertner, Samuel and John Dovidio. 2005. "Categorization, Re-categorization and Intergroup Bias" pp. 71-88 in John Dovidio, Peter Glick and Laurie Rudman (eds.) *On the Nature of Prejudice*. NY: Wiley.

Garrahan, Philip, Stewart, Paul, 1992. *The Nissan Enigma: Flexibility at Work in a Local Economy*, London: Mansell Publishing.

Garrick, Jacqueline. 2006. "The Humor of Trauma Survivors: Its Application in a Therapeutic Milieu." *Journal of Aggression, Maltreatment and Trauma* 12(1-2):169-82.

Geary, J. 1992 "Employment Flexibility and Human Resources Management: The Case of Three American Electronics Plants." *Work, Employment and Society* 6:252-70.

Gerst, Detlef, Thomas Hardwig, Martin Kuhlmann and Michael Schumann. 1999. "Group Work in the German Automobile Industry- The Case of Mercedes- Benz," pp. 366-394 in Jean-Pierre Durand, Paul Stewart, and Juan José Castillo (eds.) *Teamwork in the Automobile Industry*. London: Macmillan Press.

Goffman, Erving, 1959. *The Presentation of Self in Every Day Life*. NY: Anchor Books.

———. 1963. *Stigma*. NY: Simon & Schuster.

———. 1967. *Interaction Ritual*. NY: Pantheon Books.

Graban, Mark. 2009. *Lean Hospitals*. Boca Raton, FL: CRC Press of Taylor & Francis.

Graham, Laurie, 1995. *On the Line at Subaru-Isuzu*. Ithaca, NY: Cornell University Press.

Green, William and Yanarella, Ernest, 1996. *North American Auto Unions in Crisis: Lean Production as Contested Terrain*, Albany, NY: SUNY Press.

Grunden, Naida. 2008. *The Pittsburgh Way to Efficient Health Care: Improving Patient Care Using Toyota Based Methods*. Boca Raton, FL: CRC Press of Taylor & Francis.

Harrington, Brooke and Gary Alan Fine. 2006. "Where the Action Is: Small Groups and Recent Developments in Sociological Theory." *Small Group Research*. 37(1):4-19.

Harrison, David, Kenneth Price, Joanne Gavin and Anna Florey. 2002. "Time, Teams and Task Performance: Changing Effects of Surface- and Deep-Level Diversity on Group Functioning," *Academy of Management Journal*. 45(5):1029-45.

Henson, Kevin. 1996. *Just a Temp: Expectations and Experiences of Women Clerical Temporary Workers*. Philadelphia: Temple University Press.

Hodson, Randy. 1995. "Worker Resistance: An Underdeveloped Concept in the Sociology of Work," *Economic and Industrial Democracy*, 16:79-110.

———. 2002. "Worker Participation and Teams: New Evidence from Analyzing Organizational Ethnographies," *Economic and Industrial Democracy*, 23(4):491-528.

Homans, George. 1950. *The Human Group*, NY: Harcourt, Brace and World.

Hoschschild, Arlie. 1979. "Emotion Work, Feeling Rules, and Social Structure." *American Journal of Sociology*, 85:551-75.

House, James. 1977. "The Three Faces of Social Psychology." *Sociometry*, 40(2):161-77.

Huys, Rik, and Geert van Hootegem. 1999. "Volvo-Ghent: A Third Way?" pp. 308-324 in Jean-Pierre Durand, Paul Stewart, and Juan José Castillo (eds.), *Teamwork in the Automobile Industry: Radical Change or Passing Fashion?* London: Macmillan Press.

Ibarra, Herminia. 1995. "Race, Opportunity, and Diversity of Social Circles in Managerial Networks," *Academy of Management Journal*, 38 (3), 673-731.

Janesick, Valerie. 2000. "The Dance of Qualitative Research Design: Metaphor, Methodolatry, and Meaning," Pp. 379-400 in Norman Denzin and Yvonna Lincoln (eds.), *Handbook of Qualitative Research*, Thousand Oaks, CA: Sage Press.

Janoski, Thomas, Chrystal Grey, and Darina Lepadatu. 2007. "Do Not Pass GO: Integrating the Generalized Other and Emotions Into Theories of Difference in Symbolic Interactionism," Presented at the annual meeting of American Sociological Association, NY, August 2007.

————. 2010a. "Restoring and Extending the Generalized Other in Symbolic Interactionist Theories of Difference." Manuscript under review.

————. 2010b. "Bittersweet Emotions on the Job" Mansucript under review.

Jones, Melinda. 2002. *Social Psychology of Prejudice*. Upper Saddle River, NJ: Prentice-Hall.

Kaizen Motors. 2002. *Kaizen Motors Information Seminar* May 2002.

————. 2006. *The Kaizen Employees Handbook*, Kaizen Motors.

Kalleberg, Arne. 2000. "Nonstandard Employment Relations: Part-time, Temporary and Contract Work." *Annual Review of Sociology*, 26:341-65.

————. 2007. *The Mismatched Worker*. NY: W.W. Norton and Company.

Kalleberg, Arne, Edith Rasell, Ken Hudson, David Webster, Barbara Reskin, Naomi Cassirer, and Eileen Appelbaum. 1997. *Nonstandard Work, Substandard Jobs: Flexible Work Arrangements in the US*. Washington, DC: Economic Policy Institute.

Kalleberg, Arne, Barbara Reskin and Ken Hudson. 2000. "Bad Jobs in America: Standard and Nonstandard Employment Relations and Job Quality in the United States." *American Sociological Review*, 65(2):256-78

Kanter, Rosabeth, 1977a. "Some Effects of Proportions on Group Life: Skewed Sex Ratios and Responses to Token Women" *American Journal of Sociology* 82:965-90.

————. 1977b. *Men and Women of the Corporation*, NY: Basic Books.

Kenney, Martin and Richard Florida. 1993. *Beyond Mass Production: The Japanese System and Its Transfer to the US*, NY: Oxford University Press.

Kirkman, Bradley, Paul Tesluk and Benson Rosen. 2004. "The Impact of Demographic Heterogeneity and Team Leader-Team Member Demographic Fit on Team. Empowerment and Effectiveness." *Group and Organization Management*, 29(3):334-68.

Lattman, Peter. 2006. "Fall Out from Toyota Sexual Harassment Law Suit" May 9, 2006. *The Wall Street Journal, Digital Network*.

Lau, Dora and Keith Murnigham. 1998. "Demographic Diversity and Fault Lines: The Compositional Dynamics of Organizational Groups," *Academy of Management Review*, 23(2):325-40.

Lawrence, Paul, and Jay Lorsch. 1967. *Organization and Environment: Managing Differentiation and Integration*. Homewood, IL: Irwin Inc.

Le Naour, Jean-Yves. 2001. "Laughter and Tears in the Great War: The Need for Laughter/ The Guilt of Humour." *Journal of European Studies*. 31(3-4):265-275.

Lindquist, Jennifer H. 2004. "When Race Makes no Difference: Marriage and the Military." *Social Forces.* 83(2):731-57.

Livine-Tarandach, Reut and Jean M. Bartunek. 2009. "A New Horizon for Organizational Change." Pp. 1-36 in edited by R. Woodman, W. Pasmore and A. Shani (eds.) *Research in Organizational Change and Development* Volume 17.

MacDuffie, John and Frits Pil. 1997. "Changes in Auto Industry Employment Practices: An International Overview, pp. 9-44 in Thomas Kochan, Russell Lansbury and John MacDuffie (eds.), *After Lean Production,* Ithaca, NY: ILR Press.

Martin, Rod, Nicholas Kuiper, Joan Olinger and Kathryn Dance. 1993. "Humor, Coping with Stress, Self-Concept, and Psychological Well-Being." *Humor,* 6(1):89-104

Martin, Susan. 1999. "Police Force or Police Service? Gender and Emotional Labor," *Annals of the American Academy of Political and Social Science.*

Marx, Roberto and Mario Sergio Salerno. 1999. "Teamwork in General Motors Brazil (GMB): What Is Changing in the Organisation at Work?" pp. 151-170 in Jean-Pierre Durand, Paul Stewart, and Juan José Castillo (eds.), *Teamwork in the Automobile Industry.* London: Macmillan Press.

McAllister, Jean. 1998 "Sisyphus at Work in the Warehouse: Temporary Employment in Greenville, South Carolina," Pp. 221-242 in Kathleen Barker and Kathleen Christensen (eds.) *Contingent Work: American Employment Relations in Transition,* Ithaca, NY: ILR Press.

McDonald, Theodore, Loren Toussaint and Jennifer Schweiger. 2004. "The Influence of Social Status on Token Women Leaders' Expectations about Leading Male-Dominated Groups."*Sex Roles.* 50 (5/6).

McEvoy, Glen and Wayne Cascio. 1989. "Cumulative Evidence of the Relationship between Age and Job Performance" *Journal of Applied Psychology,* 74:11-17.

McGrath, Joseph, Holly Arrow, and Jennifer Berdahl. 2000. "The Study of Groups: Past, Present and Future," *Personality and Social Psychology Review,* 4(1):95-105.

McLeod, Poppy and Sharon Lobel. 1996. "Ethnic Diversity and Creativity in Small Groups" *Small Group Research,* 27:248-64.

Mead, George Herbert, 1967. *Mind, Self and Society,* Chicago: University of Chicago Press.

———. 1964. *Selected Writings,* NY: Bobbs-Merrill Co.

Mehri, Darius. 2005. *Notes from Toyota-land: An American Engineer in Japan.* Ithaca: ILR Press/Cornell University Press.

Milliken, F and L. Martins. 1996. "Searching for Common Threads: Understanding the Multiple Effects of Diversity in Organizational Groups." *Academy of Management Review* 21(2):402-33.

Mohrman, Susan, Susan Cohen, and Allan Mohrman. 1995. *Designing Team-Based Organizations: New Forms for Knowledge Work,* San Francisco: Jossey-Bass Publ.

Moskos, Charles and John Sibley Butler. 1996. *All that We Can Be.* NY: Basic Books.

Mueller, Charles, Ashley Finley, Roderick Iverson and James Price. 1999. "The Effects of Group Racial Composition on Job Satisfaction, Organizational Commitment and Career Commitment" *Work and Occupations* 26:187-219.

New York Times. 1999. "US and Ford Settle Harassment Case," *New York Times,* September 8, 1999.

———. 2001 "Mitsubishi Motor Settles Discrimination Lawsuit," *New York Times,* March 31, 2001.

———. 2006. "Automaker Reaches Settlement in Sexual Harassment Suit," *New York Times,* August 5, 2006.

Nissan North America, Inc. 2009. *Nissan Information Seminar,* Smyrna, Tennessee. August 2009.

Nollen, Stanley. 1996. Negative Aspects of Temporary Employment. *Journal of Labor Research.* 17(4):562-82.

Nollen, Stanley, and Helen Axel. 1996. *Managing Contingent Workers: How to Reap the Benefits and Reduce the Risks,* NY: American Management Association.

OECD. 2002. *Employment Outlook.* Paris: OECD.

Ogasawara, Yuko, 1998. *Office Ladies and Salaried Men: Power, Gender, and Work in Japanese Companies.* Berkeley, CA: University of California Press.

Osono, Emi, Norihiko Shimizu and Hirotaka Takeuchi. 2008. *Extreme Toyota: Radical Contradictions that Drive Success at the World's Best Manufacturer.* NY: Wiley.

Paletz, Susannah, Kaiping Peng, Miriam Erez and Christina Maslach. 2004. "Ethnic Composition and Its Differential Impact on Group Processes in Diverse Teams" *Small Group Research* 35(2):128-57.

Parker, Mike and Jane Slaughter. 1988. *Choosing Sides: Unions and the Team Concept,* Boston: South End Press.

Parker, Robert. 1994. *Flesh Peddlers and Warm Bodies: The Temporary Help Industry and Its Workers,* New Jersey: Rutgers University Press.

Parrish, Monique and Patricia Quinn. 1999. "Laughing Your Way to Peace of Mind: How a Little Humor Helps Caregivers Survive." *Clinical Social Work Journal.* 27(2):203-211.

Pearce, J. 1993 "Toward and Organizational Behavior of Contract Laborers: Their Psychological Involvement and Effects on Employee Coworkers." *Academy of Management Journal* 36:1082-1096.

Pelled, Lisa. 1996. "Demographic Diversity, Conflict and Work Group Outcomes: An Intervening Process Theory," *Organization Science.* 7:615-31.

Pelled, Lisa, K. Eisenhardt and K. Xin. 1999. "Exploring the Black Box: An Analysis of Work Group Diversity, Conflict, and Performance" *Administrative Science Quarterly* 44(1):1-28.

Pettigrew, Thomas. 1998. "Intergroup Contact Theory" *Annual Review of Psychology.* 49:65-85.

Pettigrew, Thomas and Linda Tropp. 2006. "A Meta-Analytic Test of Intergroup Contact Theory," *Journal of Personality and Social Psychology,* 90:751-783.

Popielarz, Pamela and Miller McPherson. 1995. "On the Edge or In Between: Niche Position, Niche Overlap and the Duration of Voluntary Memberships." *American Journal of Sociology* 101:698-720.

Powers, Daniel and Christopher Ellison. 1995. "Interracial Contact and Black Racial Attitudes: The Contact Hypothesis and Selectivity Bias," *Social Forces,* 74 (1):205-226

Pruijt, Hans, 2003. Teams Between Neo-Taylorism and Anti-Taylorism, *Economic and Industrial Democracy.* 24(1):77-101.

Ragin, Charles and Howard Becker. 1992. *What is a Case? Exploring the Foundations of Social Inquiry.* NY: Cambridge University Press.

Ragins, Belle Rose and Jorge Gonzalez. 2003. "Understanding Diversity in Organizations: Getting a Grip on a Slippery Construct," *Organizational Behavior: The State of the Science,* Mahwah, NJ: Lawrence Erlbaum.

Richards, Lyn. 2005. *Handling Qualitative Data: A Practical Guide,* Thousand Oaks, CA: Sage.

Rinehart, James, Christopher Huxley and David Robertson. 1997. *Just Another Car Factory? Lean Production and Its Discontents,* Ithaca, NY: ILR Press.

Riordan, Christine and Lynn-McFarlane Shore. 1997. "Demographic Diversity and Employee Attitudes: Examination of Relational Demography within Work Units," *Journal of Applied Psychology,* 82:342-58.

Ritzer, George. 1993. *The McDonaldization of Society.* Thousand Oaks, CA: Pine Forge Press.

Roemer, John E. 1996. *Theories of Distributive Justice.* Cambridge: Harvard University Press.

Rogers, Jackie. 1995. "Just a Temp: Experience and Structure of Alienation in Temporary Clerical Employment." *Work and Occupations* 22:137-66.

Sanders, Teela. 2004. "Controllable Laughter: Managing Sex Work through Humor." *Sociology.* 38(2):273-291.

Scheff, Thomas. 2003. "Shame in Self and Society", *Symbolic Interaction,* 26(2):239-62.

Schiappa, Edward, Peter Gregg and Dean Hewes. 2005. "The Parasocial Contact Hypothesis," *Communication Monographs,* 72(1):92-115.

Sewell, Graham. 1998. "The Discipline of Teams: The Control of Team-Based Industrial Work Through Electronic and Peer Surveillance" *Administrative Science Quarterly,* 43(2):397-428.

Shapiro, Gillian, "Employee Involvement: Opening the Diversity Pandora's Box?" *Personnel Review,* 29(3):304-323.

Silver, Allan. 1997. "The Curious Importance of Small Groups in American Sociology." in Jeffrey Alexander, Raymond Boudon, and Mohamed Cherkaoui (eds.) *The Classical Tradition in Sociology. The American Tradition* vol. III, Thousand Oaks, CA: Sage.

Simmel, Georg. 1971. *On Individuality and Social Forms* Chicago: University of Chicago Press.

Simon, Herbert. 1945. *Administrative Behavior* NY: Free Press.

Simon, Jolene. 1990. "Humor and Its Relationship to Perceived Health, Life Satisfaction and Morale in Older Adults." *Issues in Mental Health Nursing.* 11(1):17-31.

Simsarian-Webber, Sheila and Lisa Donahue. 2001. "Impact of Highly Job-Related and Less Job-Related Diversity on Work Group Cohesion and Performance: A Meta-analysis" *Journal of Management,* 27:141-162.

Sinclair, Amanda, 1992. "The Tyranny of Team Ideology," *Organization Studies,* 13(4):611-26.

Smith, Vicki, 1994. "Institutionalizing Flexibility in a Service Firm." *Work and Occupations* 21: 284-307.

———. 1997. "New Forms of Work Organizations." *Annual Review of Sociology.* 23: 315-39.

———. 1998. "The Fractured World of the Temporary Worker: Power, Participation, and Fragmentation in the Contemporary Workplace." *Social Problems,* 45(4):411-30.

———. 2001. *Crossing the Great Divide: Worker Risk and Opportunity in the New Economy.* Ithaca, NY: ILR Press.

———. 2001. "Teamwork versus Tempwork: Managers and the Dualisms of Workplace Restructuring" Pp. 7-28 in Daniel Cornfield, Karen Campbell, and Holly McCammon (eds) *Working in Restructured Workplaces: New Directions for the Sociology of Work.* Thousand Oaks, CA: Sage.

Sorensen, Jesper. 2004. "The Organizational Demography of Racial Employment Segregation," *American Journal of Sociology* 110(3):626-71.

Stake, Robert. 2000. "Case Studies," Pp. 435-454 in Norman Denzin and Yvonna Lincoln (eds.) *Handbook of Qualitative Research,* Thousand Oaks, CA: Sage Press.

Stewart, Greg and Murray Barrick. 2000. "Team Structure and Performance: Assessing the Mediating Role of Intrateam Process and the Moderating Role of Task Type," *Academy of Management Journal* 43(2):135-148.

Thomas, David and Robin Ely. 1996. "Making Differences Matter: A New Paradigm for Managing Diversity," *Harvard Business Review* (September/ October), 79-90.

Thorson, A. and F. C. Powell. 1997. "Psychological Health and Sense of Humor." *Journal of Clinical Psychology* 53(6):605-19.

Timmerman, Thomas. 2000. "Racial Diversity, Age Diversity, Interdependence, and Team Performance," *Small Group Research*, 31(5):592-606.

Toyoto Motor Manufacturing Kentucky (TMMK). 1998. *Kaizen Motors Information Seminar* Georgetown, Kentucky. May 2002.

———. 2004. *The Toyota Team Members Handbook*, Georgetown, KY: TMMK.

Tsui, Anne, Terri Egan, and Charles O'Reilly. 1992. "Being Different: Relational Demography and Organizational Attachment," *Administrative Science Quarterly* 37(4):549-80.

Tsui, Anne and Barbara Gutek. 1999. *Demographic Differences in Organizations: Current Research and Future Directions*, Lanham, Maryland: Lexington Books.

Turner, Lowell, 1991. *Democracy at Work: Changing Labor Markets and the Future of Labor Unions*. Ithaca, NY: Cornell University Press.

Turner, Lowell, Harry Katz and Richard Hurd (eds.), 2001. *Rekindling the Movement: Labor's Quest for Relevance in the Twenty-First Century* Ithaca, NY: ILR Press.

US Department of Commerce. 2005. *Statistical Abstract of the United States*. Washington, D.C.: US GP9.

US Bureau of the Census. 2005. *Supplement to the Current Population Survey*. February. www.dol.gov .

Vallas, Steven. 2003. "Why Teamwork Fails: Obstacles to Workplace Change in Four Manufacturing Plants," *American Sociological Review*, 68:223-250.

———. 2006. "Theorizing Teamwork under Contemporary Capitalism" *Research in the Sociology of Work*, Volume 16, San Diego: JAI Press.

Vallas, Steven and J. Beck. 1996. "The Transformation of Work Revisited: The Limits of Flexibility in American Manufacturing" *Social Problems*, 43(3):339-61.

Vosko, Leah. 2000. *Temporary Work: The Gendered Rise of a Precarious Employment Relationship*, Toronto: University of Toronto Press.

Wallace, Terry. 1999. "It's a Man's World!': Restructuring Gender Imbalance in the Volvo Truck Company," *Gender, Work and Organization* 6(1):20-31.

Warr, Peter. 1995. "In What Circumstances Does Job Performance Vary with Age?" In Jose M. Peiro, Melia Fernando, Jose Luis and Otto Luque (eds.), *Work and Organizational Psychology: Proceedings of the Sixth European Congress of Work and Organizational Psychology*, Hove, UK: Taylor and Francis.

Weisbord, Marvin. 2004. *Productive Workplaces Revisited: Organizing and Managing for Dignity, Meaning and Community in the 21st Century* San Francisco, CA: Jossey-Bass.

Weisenberg, M., I. Tepper, and J. Schwarzwald. 1995. "Humor as a Cognitive Technique for Increasing Pain Tolerance." *Pain* 63:207-212.

Wharton, Amy and James Baron. 1991. "Satisfaction? The Psychological Impact of Gender Segregation on Women at Work," *Sociological Quarterly*, 32:365-87.

Wharton, Amy, Thomas Rotolo and Sharon Bird. 2000. "Social Context at Work: A Multilevel Analysis of Job Satisfaction." *Sociological Forum* 15:65-90.

Williams, Christine. 1992. "The Glass Escalator: Hidden Advantages for Men in the 'Female' Professions." *Social Problems* 39: 253-67.

Williams, John and Deborah Best. 1990. *Sex and Psyche: Gender and Self Viewed Cross-*

Culturally, Newbury Park, CA: Sage.

―――. 1990. *Measuring Sex Stereotypes: A Multinational Study* Newbury Park, CA: Sage.

Williams, Katherine and Charles O'Reilly. 1998. "Demography and Diversity in Organizations: A Review of 40 Years of Research," *Research in Organizational Behavior,* 20:77-140.

Wolcott, Harry. 1994. *Transforming Qualitative Data: Description, Analysis, and Interpretation* Thousand Oaks, CA: Sage.

Womack, James P., Daniel T. Jones and Daniel Roos. 1990. *The Machine that Changed the World: The Story of Lean Production* NY: Harper-Collins.

Wright, Stephen and Norann Richard. 2010. "Cross-Group Helping: Perspectives on Why and Why not." Pp. 311-335 in Stefan Stürmer and Mark Snyder (eds.) *The Psychology of Prosocial Behavior.* Chinchester, UK: Wiley-Blackwell.

Wright, Stephen, A. Aron and L. R. Tropp. 2002. "Including Others (and Groups) in the Self." Pp. 343-63 in J. P. Forgas and K. D. Williams (eds.), *The Social Self: Cognitive, Interpersonal and Intergroup Perspectives.* Philadelphia, PA: Psychology Press.

Wright, Stephen, S. M. Brody, and A. Aron. 2005. "Intergroup Contact: Still Our Best Hope for Improving Intergroup Relations" Pp. 115-42 in *Social Psychology of Prejudice.* Seattle, WA: Lewinian Press.

Yates, Charlotte, Wayne Lewchuk and Paul Stewart. 2001. "Empowerment as a Trojan Horse: New Systems of Work Organization in the North American Automobile Industry." *Economic and Industrial Democracy.* 22(4):517-41.

Yin, Robert, 1994. *Case Study Research: Design and Method* Thousand Oaks, CA: Sage.

Chapter 1

1. Japanese transplants came to the US due to American restrictions on imports. In the 1980s, the American government under President Ronald Reagan imposed import controls on Japanese vehicles coming into the US. This caused the Japanese auto manufacturers to change strategies in two ways. They produced more luxury cars in Japan because the quotas were based on numbers of vehicles and not prices, and they decided to build automobile plants to make moderately priced cars in the US. Initially, they faced difficulties centered on bringing the Japanese style of teamwork to a country that heavily invested in individualistic values. Although American managers had some problems adjusting to Japanese methods, most workers embraced teamwork and were often dissatisfied when the full Japanese model was not implemented.

2. Wright and colleagues add "the expansion of the self" to other out-groups in their theory of contact (Wright and Richard, 2010, p. 316; Wright et al., 2005; Wright et al., 2002).

3. Of the recent meta-analysis studies on this topic, most have concluded that the findings are inconclusive on the impact of diversity in teams. This is because we still do not understand the underlying mechanisms that are in the "black box" of demography. Further, few explanatory models link diversity and performance (Simsarian Webber and Donahue, 2001; Milliken and Martins, 1996; Williams and O'Reilly, 1998; Ragins and Gonzalez, 2003; and Kirkman et al., 2004).

4. We also examined a psychological "organizational ecological" theory that incorporated consultants and managers in an organizational change exercise (Bartunek, 2003; Livine-Tarandach and Bartunek, 2009). One interesting application of the theory was done by Meg Bond at ChemPro, a pseudonym for a New England Chemical Corporation. However, this resembled a form of social psychological action research, which was not taking place at Kaizen Motors. We were explaining what had happened at Kaizen Motors and were not engaging in a change process ourselves.

5. The main difference between the Japanese and the Swedish teamwork is that in the Japanese style, the team leader takes most of the decision, while in the Swedish system, the decision-making process is more democratic and transparent (Berggren, 1993). German and the Swedish systems of production include socio-technical systems design, industrial democracy and humanization of working life (Turner, 1991). In these systems, you can find situations where all the team members can be involved in the decision-making process; they can divide the managerial responsibilities among themselves; they can rotate in the position of team leader or they can even decide to not have a leader at all (Pruijt, 2003).

6. Herbert Simon theorized about these forms of control in the 1940s with: (1) fully unobtrusive controls (where managers control the cognitive premises of action through organizational values and culture, training and indoctrination, selective hiring, and personnel rejuvenation) are the most efficient, relatively inexpensive and less resented forms of control; (2) bureaucratic unobtrusive controls as long distance but recognized controls (job specialization, organizational rules, technological and bureaucratic standardization, and assembly line technology); and (3) direct fully obtrusive controls (sanctions, orders, directives, surveillance, rules), which usually are the most expensive and most resented forms of controlling workers (1945).

7. The Saturn Division of GM had highly autonomous teams with ten to fifteen members. They planned team operations, did their own budgeting, recruited new members, managed supplies, controlled quality, and decided the rhythms of job rotation (Cornette, 1999). GM teams other than Saturn tend to have ten members, and four work units form a work unit module (Marx and Salerno, 1999). In Europe, Peugeot teams are made of thirty workers divided in three groups (Durand and Hatzfeld, 1999), Renault teams are called elementary work units and are made of ten to twenty workers (Freyssenet 1999), Fiat teams are composed of large elementary organizational units (20 to 40 workers) (Camuffo and Micelli, 1999), Volvo teams are made of ten to fifteen workers (Huys and Van Hootegem, 1999), Saab work group organizations have eight to ten members (Brulin and Nilsson, 1999), and Opel teams have sixteen employees (Albertijn et al., 1999). Mercedes-Benz teams are called self-organized work groups (Gerst et al., 1999). The traditional Fordist system does not have teams but this approach is clearly in decline.

8. Mazda did care about the health and safety of its workers. It implemented a zero-accident policy and offered a total wellness program with fitness and other programs. However in the early phase, they had more accidents and lost working days due to injuries than the average for the state of Michigan. Most of the accidents occurred by the end of the shifts (Fucini and Fucini, 1990: 178). The heat and the 57-second *takt* time took their toll on the workers. Many workers lost also a lot of weight when they adjusted to just-in-time work pace. Workers started to develop carpal syndrome only after a year and a half, and people on restriction were often ridiculed and harassed by co-workers, managers and others.

9. In the opposite direction, there was some racial harassment at these plants from the beginning. At the beginning, the Japanese were harassed by American bigots at the Mazda plant. Some construction workers wore T-shirts with a picture of the Hiroshima bomb and with a short comment: "Made in the USA, tested in Japan." Yet, as Fucini and Fucini (1990) described it, the Japanese showed no emotional response to any obscenities shouted at them, or to the racist graffiti in the restrooms. The overall community welcomed the Japanese in their town. The Japanese families received many invitations for

dinner on Thanksgiving Day or Christmas, but there were also Americans who shouted at them that "the Japanese are taking American jobs."

10. A complicating factor is that men were sometimes reluctant to report developing work injuries, which is consistent with the literature on masculinity and work.

11. Sexual harassment is not only present in Japanese transplant companies, but it exists across throughout American industry. In 1999, Ford Motor Company agreed to pay $8,000,000 in the largest settlement ever reached between the Equal Employment Opportunity Commission (EEOC) and any automobile manufacturer based in the US. Harassment did not stop though and Ford was sued again by EEOC in 2001. The Chrysler Plant in Toledo has had similar complaints.

12. The surveys revealed a substantial number of native-Americans, which we initially found quite puzzling. However, it turned out that many white workers were identifying themselves as native-Americans as opposed to being Japanese.

Chapter 3

1. In *Team Toyota*, Besser (1996) includes an interesting chapter on the women of Toyota, which briefly deals with the experiences of women on the line, and focuses more on the experiences of the invisible Toyota women, the wives of the Japanese managers.

2. This does not mean that the work is not hard. One woman in the study said "It's hard to be a woman and to work here. . . . I had some . . . problems . . . because you need a lot of upper body strength." But given that those women and men have the strength to make it, being a good worker then depends on other factors.

3. One team member, who was the only man in a team with four women, criticized team leaders. He said that he would not help women more than he would help men because men and women get the same pay. The years spent in his female team made him draw the conclusion that women receive help quicker if they have an injury and that team leaders tend to babysit them.

4. Some men gave a stereotypical interpretation of gender roles to their explanations. For instance, some men say that women have safer behavior at work because of their experience with raising children. As one team member puts it, women are more careful with accidents because their primary role at home is to be caretakers. His perception is that women have a motherly intuition for safety, which they carry with them at work.

5. Multiple selves suggest intersectional theory (Collins 1986, 2000; Crenshaw, 1991). However, our emphasis lies in how team identity becomes stronger than other identities. This mitigates against using this approach on a consistent basis. Nonetheless, our division of diversity into four components (gender, race, age, and temporary status) cannot avoid intersectionality in the sense of a number of overlaps, which we discuss in this study.

6. Some Japanese auto companies have bad reputations on gender equality and sexual harassment. A recent opinion survey at the Toyota Nizumi plant in Japan showed that 75% of the women and 62% of the men surveyed said that they knew of someone who had experienced sexual harassment on the plant. Most of the harassment incidents involved rude jokes and sexually oriented questions, 25% involved being touched, and 4% of the women said that they have been forced to have sex with a superior (Mehri, 2005).

7. Many Japanese women in their homeland still assume the servant role of office ladies and are not assigned important jobs according to their credentials. During his three

years of participant observation at Nizumi plant in Japan, Mehri (2005) noticed that Toyota women have a double mandate: they are supposed to do the job as well as men, and they are supposed to display their femininity. "Being the flower of the shop" meant that the assembly line girl should try hard to look attractive, popular, sensitive, interested in homemaking, religion, and the traditional Japanese customs.

Chapter 4

1. Men may also have improved self confidence because of their weight loss, but we would contend that, while not unimportant, appearance is less critical to men's sense of self. For example, women are more likely to buy diet products than men, and anorexia and bulimia are rare among males.

2. One wonders if Dwight is aware of the high divorce rate at Kaizen Motors, and that he is pre-empting the possibility of an affair. On the other hand, it is possible that Dwight is simply a husband more sensitive than most.

Chapter 5

1. In this chapter, we concentrate on African-Americans. Middle-Eastern and Hispanic workers were distinct minorities who fit into Kaizen Motors less well than others. They most probably fit into token positions. Kahlid, a 21-year old temp, originally from the Middle East, is described by his team members like somebody who "tries to fit in" and who "you can tell he wants to be one of the guys." Of course, this desire of fitting in is exacerbated by his temporary employment status. Kahlid lived in the US since he was two years old and does not feel different than any other member of his team. But he says that the only element of diversity he brings to the team is ethnic food. Xavier, a Hispanic team leader, confessed that he also feels that he does not bring anything unique to the group and that he blends in nicely with the group. Xavier's subordinates become aware of his Hispanic heritage only when he brought Mexican food to diversity lunches (an event where team members bring different ethnic food to work). These lunches are very enjoyable activities for team members and one of the few diversity activities that they recalled during the interviews. Some team members mentioned that they even have a *Diversity Cookbook*.

Chapter 7

1. The UAW has had a consistent policy against temporary workers and dual wage structures. However, in its May 2008 collective bargaining round it agreed to a dual wage structure paying lower wages to new workers.

2. There are a number of different kinds of temporary workers. In this chapter we mainly discuss temporary workers who are eligible to obtain full-time employment. There are college students, part-time workers, and family members of workers at Kaizen who obtain temporary jobs. However, for them it is clear that in their present status, they will never be hired on for a full-time and permanent job. Also, cafeteria and other service jobs are subcontracted without the possibility of being hired on a full-time basis. Thus, this chapter refers to temporary workers who could become full-time and permanent Kaizen workers.

3. There are a number of biases operating here. For permanent team members there is a "nostalgia bias" that comes from their satisfaction from leaving temp status and gaining more job security. Hence, they say that being a temp was not so bad. We cannot control this bias. For the current temp worker there is a "fear bias" because he/she does not want management to find out that he/she is unhappy and consequently destroy his/her own chances for being hired as a permanent worker. This is also a difficult bias to control. For employees who were injured, there can be a bias against the company that injured them. In this case we found one former worker who had to hire a lawyer and fight for benefits, and he was still mad four years after leaving Kaizen Motors. However, we interviewed woman with a serious injury who had nothing but good things to say about Kaizen Motors. For former employees, there is often an "émigré bias" (from the Soviet émigré literature when interviews could not be done in the USSR) whereby the most dissatisfied employees are leaving. They tend to criticize the organization for which they had worked. However, aside from the worker who had to hire a lawyer, these workers were largely positive toward the company. Consequently, we cannot solve all of these biases, but the last one seems rather convincing in that it is opposite to the expected disgruntled response and it operates in Kaizen Motors' favor. Nonetheless, permanent and former workers did make many comments about how being a temp was difficult and unpleasant.

Conclusion

1. From a methodological point of view, the study may have revealed a loyalty bias of team members to protect the image of their own groups and teams. However, workers spoke enthusiastically about teamwork in general and about their positive and negative experiences of working in other teams.

INDEX

A

accidents, 138, n.8, 139, n. 18 (see injuries)
Adler, Paul, 3, 10
affair, extra-marital, xi, 13, 17, 26, 43, 47-58, 113, 114, 118, 140, n.21
age, 3-7, 12, 16, 17, 21, 31, 52, 59-60, 63, 65, 70-74, 81-94, 95, 102, 112, 115, 116-117, 120-21
Allport, Gordon, 6, 7, 62, 113
andon cord, 11, 20, 28, 42
Appelbaum, Eileen, 3, 10
automobile companies (see Chrysler, Ford, GM, Honda, Nissan, Mazda, Mercedes-Benz, Subaru-Isuzu, Suzuki, Toyota, and Volvo)

B

Bacharach, Samuel, 5
Baron, James, 26
Bartunek, Jean, 137, n.4
Batt, Rosemary, 10
Becker, Howard, 21

Berggren, Christian, 11, 137 n.5
Besser, Terry, 3, 9, 10, 25, 26, 46, 47, 113, 139, n.13
Bird, Sharon, 60
Blumer, Herbert, 6
Bonilla-Silva, Eduardo, 65, 71, 78
Bond, Meg, 20, 137, n.4
Braverman, Harry, xi
Burawoy, Michael, 21
Butler, John S., 79

C

CAMI (Canadian Automotive Manufacturing, Inc.), 10, 11, 14, 15, 82
Carpal tunnel syndrome, 14, 40, 82, 138 n.8
Chalice, Robert, 2
Chattopadhyay, Prithviraj, 26
ChemPro, 20, 137, n.4
Chrysler, 138, n.11, 149
Collins, Patricia Hill. 139 n.17
contact hypothesis, revised, 6-9, 46, 57, 62-63, 78, 94, 113-114, 117

About the Authors

Darina Lepadatu is the associate director of the Ph.D. program in International Conflict Management and assistant professor of sociology at Kennesaw State University in Atlanta, Georgia. Her research interests are in the areas of sociology of work and organizations (conflicts generated by gender, racial and age dynamics in the workplace), race and ethnicity (racial and ethnic conflicts, discrimination against minority groups, hate crimes against immigrants) and comparative sociology (post-communist societies, Eastern Europe). Dr. Lepadatu's teaching interests include the sociology of work and organizations, general research methods and especially advanced qualitative research methods, race and ethnicity, and the management of non-profit organizations. Her most recent publications focused on issues related to diversity and teamwork in the workplace, the discrimination of Roma in European Union, and immigration to Europe versus United States. Prior to moving to the United States, she served as European integration specialist in the Romanian Ministry of Education and Research, and participated in international missions and conferences in more than 20 countries. Dr. Lepadatu continues her collaboration with Thomas Janoski as a co-principal investigator on a National Science Foundation research grant entitled "Lean Production in Japanese Transplants and American Auto Plants: Processes of Management Control and Worker Identity in Causing Stress."

Thomas Janoski is a professor of sociology at the University of Kentucky. Earlier in his career he was a piston-shooter on the flat-head-six engine assembly line at the Chrysler Corporation Engine Plant in Trenton, Michigan. Since then he has taught work and occupations, political sociology, and comparative/historical methods at the University of California at Berkeley, Duke University, and the University of Kentucky. He is a co-principal investigator with Darina Lepadatu on the National Science Foundation project." Dr. Janoski is currently working on a new project called "The Vortex of Labor: The Impact of Outsourcing, Lean Production and Information Technology on Unemployment." He is the author of *The Ironies of Citizenship: Naturalization and Integration in Industrialized Countries* (Cambridge University Press, 2010); *Citizenship and Civil Society* (Cambridge University Press, 1998), and *The Political Economy of Unemployment: Active Labor Market Policy in the United States and West Germany* (University of California Press, 1990). He is also co-editor of *The Handbook of Political Sociology* (Cambridge University Press, 2005), and *The Comparative Political Economy of the Welfare State* (Cambridge, 1994).